W9-BRH-726

Holiday Lights!

Holiday Lights!

Brilliant Displays to Inspire Your Christmas Celebration

BY DAVID SEIDMAN

Storey Publishing

The mission of Storey Publishing is to serve our customers by publishing practical information that encourages personal independence in harmony with the environment.

Edited by Dianne Cutillo and Nancy W. Ringer
Designed by Wendy Palitz and Melanie Jolicoeur
Cover photograph by Steve Hamblin /Alamy
Back cover photographs by © Reuters NewMedia, Inc./CORBIS (top left),
© Buddy Mays/CORBIS (top right), © Photodisc/Getty (bottom left), and Ed Judice (bottom right)
Interior photo credits given on page 180
Photo research by Minda Noveck and Melanie Jolicoeur
Full-color illustrations by © Jim Lange/Retro Reps
Line drawings in chapter 5 by Brigitta Fuhrmann
Indexed by Eileen Clawson

Printed in the United States by R. R. Donnelley
10 9 8 7 6 5 4 3

Library of Congress Cataloging-in-Publication Data

Seidman, David, 1958–
Holiday lights! / David Seidman.
p. cm.
Includes index.
ISBN 1-58017-508-2 (alk. paper)
1. Christmas decorations—United States. 2. Christmas lights—United States.
I. Title.

TT900.C4S38 2003
747'.93—dc21

2003050560

Dedication

To Dawn Shannon, in hopes that her next home
will be as glorious as the ones in this book.

Acknowledgments

Boy, did I have fun writing this book. A lot of the fun is due to the people listed below.

I'm grateful to all holiday lights enthusiasts, especially those who have documented their displays with words and pictures on the Internet. A special thanks goes to Chuck Smith, whose PlanetChristmas website is a nexus for lighters everywhere.

Thanks as well to the people whom I interviewed, including Bill Clot, Mike Gaddy, Sue Hahn, Drew Hickman, Ron Max, Sally Teixeira, Peter Reed, and Steve Wisniewski, and to those who got in touch via e-mail, including Josh Barnett, Kathy Byrd, Donny Counts, Jason Emerick, Jackie Monkhouse, Greg Parcell, and Travis Wetherington.

I wouldn't have written this book if not for editor Dianne Cutillo, who hired me and, despite immense deadline stresses, was constantly helpful and patient. When Dianne left the book, she passed it to Nancy Ringer, who was always available to offer aid, guidance, and words of good cheer. Good editors are hard to find, and these two are very, very good.

Most people who see this book will probably pay more attention to the visuals than the words. That's as it should be, because the visuals are terrific. Melanie Jolicoeur and Minda Novek rounded up the stellar photographs. With photos in hand, designers Wendy Palitz and Melanie Jolicoeur took my text and created something gorgeous. And the illustrations by Jim Lange and Brigitta Fuhrmann added a little extra sparkle.

And finally, my greatest thanks and much love go to the people who drove my siblings and me around Los Angeles to see the lights every December: my parents, Marvin and Seena Seidman.

Contents

Blue Nights

One wonders whether holiday lighting began in this vein, a ward against the dark night for a home tucked in a blanket of snow.

ONE WAY

City Lights Today, as evidenced in the streets of New York *(above)* and in Rockefeller Center *(left))*, holiday lighting is a part of metropolitan culture, as much so as holiday traffic.

Even Here . . .

Even in the far-off reaches of the Mojave Desert, an isolated home shares in the global phenomenon that holiday lights have become.

135

PARKING
TO LET
WESTMORLAND HOUSE

Culture Clash

America is famous for flaunting flashiness, while England is better known for its reserve. But both go wild for holiday lights, as these displays in Las Vegas *(far left)* and London *(above)* demonstrate.

Snowless Wonders The lighting fad has spread from depths of the Northern winter to the tropical beaches of Miami, Florida *(above),* and the warm desert nights of Santa Fe, New Mexico *(right).*

97

Blazing Symbols

Across the continent, individual displays of holiday extravagance — say, for example, a gazebo *(at left)* or a caboose *(below)* — have become the pride and joy of their neighborhood, the annual icons of the season.

Okay, let's face it. These things are just plain weird — but they're Good Weird.

Good Weird is an attitude of "Yeah, this is wacky, but I like it," freak flag a-flying. Good Weird cares more about fun than about dignity. Good Weird is personal and quirky, even bizarre, but not out to hurt anyone.

Good Weird is the Sydney Opera House, with its sweeping winglike protrusions. It's the Watts Towers, one man's expression of glory made of cement and old bottles, and St. Basil's Cathedral in Moscow, with its colorful, turnip-topped domes.

Good Weird is the home of the Wills family in Mendota Heights, Minnesota, which features more than 150 illuminated candy canes. It's the 37th Street neighborhood of Austin, Texas, home to such lit-up Christmas displays as the history of evolution, a skeleton in a Santa hat behind the wheel of a Volkswagen, and Barbie riding a pink flamingo. It's the shopping districts in London that have proudly hung lights shaped like everything from moon rockets (in 1969) to tightrope-walking jugglers to polka-dot horses with candelabra antlers.

You want Good Weird on a grand scale? Take a look at Bull Run Park in Centreville, Virginia, where two miles of lights and two hundred displays include "Planet Holiday," in which aliens celebrate Christmas. Visit Jones Beach on Long Island, New York, whose more than one hundred displays include dancing fish in Santa hats. Head over to Marble Falls, Texas, where virtually the whole town has dedicated itself to light arrays that show (among other things) Santa piloting a steamship, water skiing, flying a plane and twirling a lariat that spells out MERRY TEXMAS Y'ALL.

Small versions of Good Weird have been visible on the lanes of Boston's Milky Way bowling alley, whose manager has lined them with Christmas lights, gutter

Leaders in Light

In the city or in the country, whether water-skiing Santa down farm furrows or beaming signals of lord-knows-what to the dark skies, holiday lighting fanatics around the world hold aloft the guiding torch of Good Weird.

balls be danged. It's been on a farm between Nashville and Lebanon, Tennessee, where lights have lined the furrows of plowed fields. It's been on a Menorah Helmet worn by Evanston (Illinois) Bike Club member Dave Barish.

Part of Good Weird is an attitude that says, "Stare all you want." Uniformed men shoo people away from plenty of other events that draw crowds, like celebrity-filled galas or grisly crime scenes, but light displays are friendly. Like young girls in their first fancy dresses, they want everyone to admire them. Light-crazed neighborhoods from Seattle to Miami have become famous destinations for people who like to stare at anything wild. In Texas, Virginia, and other states, whole groups of adjacent cities get together to create Trail of Lights events: routes running from one town's best displays to the best of the next town.

Some places, naturally, are more lights-mad than others. Maryland does more with light than Ohio, even though Ohio has more than twice as many people and almost four times as much land. Denver and Atlanta have a richer, more spectacular variety of lights than San Francisco, Philadelphia, or Detroit. Germany has more and bigger displays than Italy or Spain. Hong Kong, where most people are Taoist, Buddhist, or atheist, boasts grander Christmas displays than some Christian countries. So does Japan. Only God knows why; maybe the reticent Christian nations should get with the fun.

Of course, lights aren't just a Christmas thing. The Nepalese of Kathmandu light rows of yak-butter lamps to commemorate the triple anniversary of the Buddha's enlightenment, birth, and death. Moslems in Jerusalem string up lights to celebrate Ramadan. Among Jews around the world, Hanukkah is the festival of lights, and giant, electrified menorahs stand in cities with large Jewish populations — and

sometimes small ones. Galveston Island, Texas, for example, has only two synagogues but has erected a giant menorah surrounded by Stars of David as part of its Moody Gardens Festival of Lights.

Israel, fittingly, has what has been called the world's biggest menorah. Located near the town of Latrun, home of a Trappist monastery and a museum devoted to Israel's armored military corps, the metal monster stands well over 60 feet tall and weighs more than 18 tons. A construction crane lifts the rabbis who light the brute's candles, even though other rabbis have said that Jewish law and tradition discourage menorahs of such a monstrous size.

In any event, lighting on a big scale is primarily a Christmas tradition, and in many ways an American one. Lighting up stores for the holidays is fairly common in Europe, and householders in Canada, England, and Australia have been known to blind a neighbor or two — but most of the wildest displays are in the U.S.A.

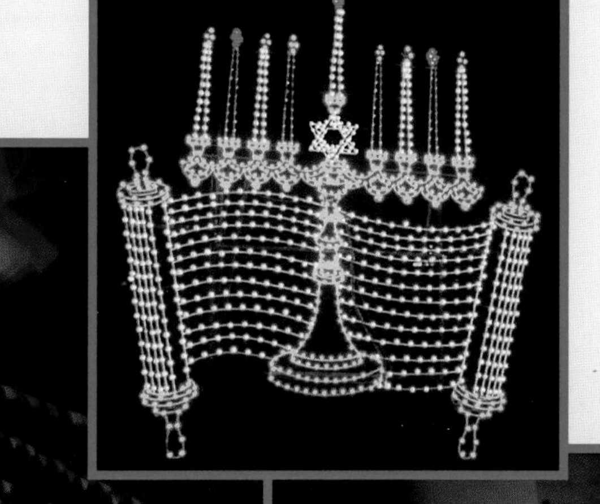

In the Beginning

"Long before there was Christianity, there were celebrations of light during the darkest days of the year," according to Stephen Nissenbaum, a University of Massachusetts at Amherst history professor and Christmas expert. "The idea of lights has more to do with the winter solstice [than with Christmas]."

The solstice — the longest night of the year — comes in late December. On the night of the solstice, called "yula" or "yule," the ancient Anglo-Saxons of northwest

The Glowing Globe

Across the world, lights blaze in celebration of the holidays, whether arches of angels for Christmas, yak butter lamps for Buddha Jayanti *(left, left inset,* and *above),* electric menorahs for Hanukkah *(right inset),* or bottles of lights for New Year's *(far right).*

Germany (and eventually, southeastern England) tried to summon the seemingly lost light by burning a slab of wood that they called a yule log. Later, they decorated a living log — that is, a tree — with lit candles. Though this tradition was dangerous (some of the trees undoubtedly caught fire), the tradition continued anyhow, as the lit-up yule log became the elaborately decorated Christmas tree.

In the mid-1800s, new technology allowed people to switch from candles to gas tubes. But the real innovation came after 1879, when Thomas Edison invented the light bulb. One of his company's executives, Edward Johnson, took some lights home in 1882 and put them on his own Christmas tree. A newspaper report called the result "a twinkling of dancing colors." Edison saw money in the practice and started making and selling electric lights specially made for the holidays. When President Grover Cleveland put electric lights on the White House Christmas tree in 1895, the whole country took notice.

By the birth of the twentieth century, lights spread from trees to walls. Big-city retail stores started the trend, using lights to decorate their windows and grab customers' attention.

But the front yards of homes weren't lit for display. For one thing, most of the country hadn't been electrified yet. What's more, the lights burned out quickly; keeping them lit all night, every night from Thanksgiving to New Year's, was pretty much out of the question. And at $12.00 per strand — a week's salary for millions of Americans — lights were too expensive for most households. People who wanted to decorate electrically usually rented lights.

The situation started to change in the 1920s, when equipment costs began to fall and more of the country began to electrify. Still, only in the 1940s did electricity become truly universal in America. And only after World War II, sometimes decades after, did people start stringing lights over their roofs and outside walls.

Even large, public institutions took their time getting into the game. It wasn't until 1968, for instance, that the Indianapolis Zoo became America's first animal park to decorate its grounds with lights and turn them into a holiday attraction.

These days, advances in mechanical engineering and chemistry have created filaments that last much longer than lights of previous generations. Computers have allowed light enthusiasts to program light sculptures to move in unexpected ways. And displays that would have awed crowds decades ago are now within the reach of any householder with enough time and cash.

Dedication and Devotion

Minami International Corporation, a leading supplier of lights, estimates that about eighty million homes get decorated with lights. Every year, householders buy more than 150 million light sets. And they put

The National 'Do-It-Yourself' Magazine – 3rd. Issue
DECEMBER 1955
1/-
The PRACTICAL HOUSEHOLDER
Editor: F. J. CAMM

History Looms Large

In 1956 London *(at right)*, workers reach up to fasten globes to one of the large Christmas lanterns that were then erected in Regent Street.

them everywhere, not just on their houses. Light enthusiasts hang bulbs on animals, oil derricks, bicycles, and food.

Driving the Light

Why do people do it? What urge makes them spend weeks designing elaborate displays, wiring their home, running up huge electric bills, and sometimes annoying the neighbors?

Some people say that holiday lights are a reaction to the tension and structure of our times. By this theory, lights decorators are rebels and artists standing up for free expression, no matter how bizarre the results might look. As novelist and journalist Emily Prager wrote in *Newsday* during the 2000 holiday season, "Holiday decorating is the last, unstructured creativity left to us."

Others feel that lights are what they were during the days of the original yule logs: a way to defy the darkness, to bring warmth and light to cold winter nights. Some even see it in sociological terms. Joseph Boskin, director of Boston University's urban studies program, has pointed out that in neighborhoods recovering from serious crime waves, "[holiday lights] demonstrate a lack of fear and say that things have calmed down."

The lighters themselves don't get so philosophical. Mostly, they say that they put up lights on their homes because they always liked seeing the displays on other homes. As Andy Jezioro, whose house in Manassas, Virginia, boasts tens of thousands of lights, has admitted, "It's kind of a childhood fantasy to have a house with lights on it. My parents would take us to see the houses with lights, and we never had the opportunity to decorate our house because we always rented."

Others decorate their homes as an act of religious exaltation, a 90-amp way of paying witness. In the Minneapolis suburb of Plymouth, Minnesota, the unabashedly devout Tim and Cathy Fischer have set up a *Peanuts* Nativity pageant and lights that remind visitors, "Jesus is the reason for the season." As Tim says, "Growing up, we lived across the street from our church, which had an outdoor nativity scene. In decorating the house, [my father's] philosophy was 'no Santa Claus.' The reason was that he didn't want the Christian Nativity scene on one side of the street, and the 'secular scene' on the other side . . . I've adopted the philosophy of keeping the true meaning of Christmas in our displays ever since. You'll never see any generic 'Season's Greetings' or 'Happy Holidays' signs at our house, although you'll find a large 'Merry Christmas.'"

And of course, many lighters plug in for the expressions they see when visitors catch sight of a wild extravaganza of bulbs. "I love seeing the families in their cars with the kids and the blankets in the back seat," Jezioro has said. "It just does something to them, kind of a relaxed feeling," observed Joe Lassiter from Hillsborough, North Carolina, who has put up everything from skating penguins to more than a dozen trees with a thousand lights each.

Light Power

The power of light to make people happy is no small thing. In the early 1990s, Texas pilot John Butler wanted to do something for kids who were desperately ill, so he started a nonprofit organization called Fly the Kids. From 1993 through 2000, Fly the Kids took more than 40,000 children up in helicopters or small planes for aerial tours of the holiday lights. Local pilots and crew members volunteered to man the flights.

Lights can even bring true love. In Austin's wildly lit 37th Street neighborhood, a friend of resident Jamie Lipman brought another friend, Sharon Smith, to see the lights. Something happened between Sharon and Jamie that was brighter than the bulbs. Within three months, the two were married.

Then there's Greg Metzger of Santa Barbara, California. In 2000, he arranged holiday lights on his home to spell out "Will you marry me?" as his proposal to his girlfriend, Keri Hall. "Just in case Hall missed the point, Metzger dropped to one knee to repeat the proposal," reported the Associated Press. "She answered, 'Yes, of course.'"

In the holiday season of 2001, Liz Sulik wanted to cheer up the people of the Rockaways, a peninsula on Long Island. So did KeySpan Corporation, the area's largest distributor of natural gas. The Rockaways had lost more than 100 people in the terrorist attacks on September 11 and even more when an American Airlines plane crashed into the peninsula's south coast. To alleviate the residents' gloom, KeySpan and Sulik, president of the Rockaways' Chamber of Commerce, chose holiday lights. To that end, KeySpan gave the Chamber $20,000, which Sulik used to string up lights in locations all over the peninsula.

Speaking of money, plenty of lighters set up a coin box on the premises and use

The Red & Green Monster **Fifty-two stories high, the imposing Terminal Tower in Cleveland is a singular monument to the colors of Christmas.**

their displays to attract donations for favorite charities. For more than 30 years, the Cripps Place neighborhood of Fremont, California, has raised money for the Lymphoma and Leukemia Society. Tom and Linda Chilcote of San Jose, California, used their lit-up home as a donation station for the Second Harvest Food Bank (America's largest hunger-relief group) and collected more than 1,000 pounds of edibles.

Even big institutions use lights to make money. The Miller Funeral Home in Black Mountain, North Carolina, has sold limousine tours of holiday lights, with the proceeds donated to the local police. In Huntington, Indiana, the Parkview Huntington Hospital Foundation set up the Holiday Lights for Health, a charity in which each contribution nets the donor "a light or lights displayed throughout the holiday season; tribute cards sent to those you honor or memorialize telling them of your gift [in their name]; an invitation to a lighting ceremony; [and] your name in the lighting ceremony program." In 2001, the hospital raised $45,000.

The Lights in the Parkway display of Allentown, Pennsylvania, is so popular that the city is able to deploy the display's admission fees to help pay for city parks. (The display also provides "PR that we couldn't buy if we wanted to," Community and Economic Development Director Ed Pawlowski has said.)

Neola, Iowa (population 894), values lights so much that in 2002, the city paid its residents for lighting their homes. The city decreed that householders who decorated their homes with lights would get a discount of 25 percent off their power bill. The idea was to get everyone to participate in the town's old-fashioned Christmas celebration, which the city saw as a big draw for tourist dollars.

The Never-Ending Story

In the future, maybe lights will go wireless or arrange themselves courtesy of artificial intelligence. Or maybe they won't. It doesn't matter. Today's displays are amazing enough.

So are the stories of how and why the people involved put them together.

The Merry Caravan **Although it will have to leave the tree behind, this vehicle can carry the rest of its display with it.**

North Pole

Individual Effort

Lighting up homes lights up faces. Kids' faces. Grown-ups' faces. Even, occasionally, a curmudgeonly Scrooge's face. It's a glorious explosion of individual creativity and personal style, from overblown to elegant and everything in between. Here are the stories of some of the masters who use lights — and cartoon characters, computer animation, music, and more — to turn their homes into scenes of holiday splendor. It takes time, money, and massive effort. But the lights-masters wouldn't have it any other way.

God bless the independent individual. Call him an extroverted show-off, a quirky eccentric, or just nuts, he gleefully exposes his obsessions for the world to see and refuses to let the opinions of the small-minded and cantankerous slow him down. He makes his home a spectacle, filling the air with a garish glow, sentimental tunes, and funky sculptures that dance courtesy of computerized motion control.

And sometimes, his name is Clot.

The Lord of Lights

The first thing to understand is that Bill Clot is not insane. A father, a husband for more than 40 years, and a responsible executive in the aircraft industry, he seems as solid and unremarkable as any other successful man. But for decades, this homeowner in Pinecrest, Florida, has erected one of the world's biggest single-family light arrays. With more than 600,000 light bulbs over the family's 50,000-square-foot property, "It literally looks like daylight," Clot's son Josh told CNN. "We decorate every tree that can be seen."

And not just the trees. With the jovial and generous Bill in charge of the design and the well-organized Josh supervising the construction, the Clots have created and lit more than 100 animated figures. Ice-skating penguins glide along a frozen pond (made of plywood and foil-backed canvas) as a sea lion sticks his head up through the ice. Toy soldiers, as tall as a full-grown man, stand guard over a scene from *The Nutcracker*. Toy trains circle a miniature village on more than 700 feet of track. Santa stands at the North Pole, elves feed reindeer in a barn, a band of animal musicians perform, and Dickensian characters deliver gifts, sing carols, and sell apples and chestnuts.

For the thousands of people who have seen the display, the results have been stunning — literally. "The older men would [go into a] trance and walk into cars," Clot says, "and grown women would cry." And they've come by the drove: Every year, Clot gives out more than 50,000 candy canes to visitors. The display has even become nationally famous. In 2002, NBC's *Today* show decreed it the best in the country.

Clot can't exactly account for why he does light up so big. Certainly, Christmas was always an important and festive time in his family while he was growing up in the 1930s; and as he got older, he studied electronics and worked for his father, who owned a company that rewound electric motors. Still, he didn't go in for flashy electrical effects on his home until the early 1980s. "One year, I got an opportunity to buy a thousand sets of lights wholesale, like 70 cents a set for a 50-light set, and that's when I started going real big with it," he says. From then on, he says, "It sort of grew like Topsy." To *Today*'s Al Roker, he confessed, "It's a sickness. You get one light and you say, 'more, more, more.'"

Lots more. Clot estimates that he uses about 500 extension cords. He put power centers and breakers outside his garage, avoiding the inconvenience of running thick cords from every plug inside the house through every window to the outdoors. To get the vibrant glare that has made his home famous, he says, "The whole secret is not only the amount of lights, but also the layering of lights — having a row of lights beyond a row of lights." Naturally, his December light bill runs into the thousands of dollars.

Before you think of scolding Clot for using up electricity, you should know that he uses his awesome powers for good. Through donation boxes at the display, the Clot family has raised nearly $400,000 from visitors and given it to the Woman's Cancer Association at the University of Miami. "We have nights where we get $2,500 to $3,000 in the boxes," he says.

CLOT'S ARMY

Creating the Clot family's display (pictured at right) in Pinecrest, Florida, takes more than a dozen volunteers. Many of them are children. "I've got a bunch of real good kids who start coming over here about the time they're 10 . . . By 12 or 13, they become really into it. Then they get to be 15 or 16, they discover cars and girls, and they're gone," Bill Clot says.

Unlike other lighters, who need weeks to assemble their displays, Bill says that he and his helpers put up his cornucopia in about five days, starting the Sunday before Thanksgiving, and take it down in two. To drape lights in trees and on the house, he rents two bucket trucks. "We get a 45-footer and a 60-footer."

For the future, Clot says, "I would like to get more moving stuff" — in other words, more figures that move — "but it just gets harder to do."

Does he ever expect to stop doing it? "Yeah. When they put me in a box."

Big Tree, Big Fun

Who needs Douglas fir? Lighting Florida's indigenous trees *(left)* works for Bill Clot.

Hello, Frosty This jolly chap stands at Ron Lister's display in Florida. Lister has 20,000 bulbs in his display, including some that flash in rhythm to music.

Home, Bright Home

Bill Clot may be the most renowned of home lighters, but others don't do so badly. Bob and Judy Henthorne of St. Paul, Minnesota, are said to have had more than 200 lighted figures on display. About 25 miles to the northeast, in New Scandia Township, Jim and Bruce Johnson have 1,000 animated figures and more than 300,000 lights on their three-acre spread, which they surround with 130 lighted candy canes. In Prairie Village, Kansas, retired phone-company employee Mike Babick has more than 1,000 animated characters. And Michael Albritton of Atlanta claims more than a million lights on his two-acre parcel; he brings in professional designers and a construction crew to put them up, a process that takes two months and costs about $50,000.

Then there are Bill and Peg Chartres of Lobethal, South Australia. Lobethal is a small town with fewer than 2,000 people, but it throws a Christmas Lights Festival every year. Since 1988, the Chartreses' light show has been one of the season's highlights. An estimated quarter of a million people visit the display every year, an especially impressive statistic given that the entire population of South Australia is only about 1.5 million.

The Chartreses' house is home to hundreds of wooden cutouts, many of which they make themselves. The front of the house features almost every Christmas

symbol you can imagine: candles, trees, bells, stars, candy canes, toys (including a jack-in-the-box with a North Pole elf springing out), a caroling choir (including a pipe organist), and Nativity scenes, complete with camels. Santa and his reindeer are on the roof and throughout the property. (For the truly obsessed light decorator, there may be only one God, but there are lots of Santas.) Also on the roof, just below a large, lighted NOEL, is an enormous, incongruous star of David. Even the Charteses' dog, a white Staffy cross named Princess, is lit up; her collar carries flashing lights.

Inside the Chartreses' house, visitors will find the Christmas room. On a staircase stand miniature snowmen, carolers, churches, and houses. Elsewhere in the room is a tiny store labeled "Christmas Shop," with a wreath on the door, Christmas stockings in the window, and Santa and his reindeer on the roof. The room also contains dozens of Christmas trees, ranging in size from tiny to full-sized, plus strands of tinsel, a miniature carousel, and additional Santas and reindeer. Unlike the outside lights, which are a seasonal thing, the Christmas room stays set up all year.

Like the Clots, Bill and Peg Chartres have used their lights to attract donations. In 2001, for instance, they raised $1,800 for cancer research and $330 for victims of a nearby fire.

Better Big

In 1987, Andy and Barbara Jezioro of Virginia had only five or six strings of light on their house *(above)*. Now look.

Cost Consciousness

Lighting up a house can get very expensive. In Anchorage, Alaska, Brian Cain's 100-plus figures — including a Nativity scene and Disney figures — more than double his light bill to about $400 per month. In Tewksbury, Massachusetts, Joe Lester's display of more than 100,000 lights, plus reindeer with moving heads, a helicopter caught in a tree, and a train on the roof, raises his bill by even more.

These two are pikers compared to John Sesso of Old Bridge, New Jersey. His display employs more than 50,000 lights, a giant American flag, a Star of David, a dreidel, gingerbread men, airplanes, a snowman, a huge stocking, candy canes, a locomotive, and toy soldiers more than seven feet tall, and reportedly it has cost him as much as $700 to light for a single month. And in Sunrise, Florida, a few hundred miles north of Bill Clot's spectacular show, Jason Wade and Ed Bussiere — a water-treatment plant employee and a cop, respectively — say that they've spent up to $10,000 per year on decorations, plus more than $1,000 in electric bills. But then, their array includes model trains, seventeen Christmas trees, miniature villages with hundreds of houses (including Elvis Presley's Graceland), a snowmaking machine, Santa's Workshop in the garage, and hundreds of thousands of lights.

The king of big-spending light madmen may have been Emilio Palmero. He wasn't a rich man. He was an Italian immigrant with an eighth-grade education who worked in a bakery. Still, when he visited foreign countries he looked for new items to light up. His home in Burien, Washington, sported more than 100,000 lights shining on Snoopys, Santas, snowmen, and reindeer; all told, the display raised his light bill for the season to as much as $4,500.

Friendly Feud

Minneapolis neighbors offer competing shows, one with a neon Nativity and the other with sheer bulb volume. In Burbank, the Laprath *(left inset)* and Norton *(right inset)* homes deliver ever wilder spectacles.

Bizarreness in Burbank

While the Chartreses spread their display over a sprawling lot, Dick Norton of Burbank, California, crams his onto his front lawn until the hundreds of animated figures and thousands of lights pile over each other in frenzied, magnificent chaos.

Bart Simpson and Kermit the Frog plush dolls ride a nearly full-sized merry-go-round that revolves as its horses rise and dip. Near the merry-go-round, so close that collisions seem imminent, animated wooden children go up and down on a four-seat teeter-totter, their legs actually pushing off the ground whenever they touch down. A Ferris wheel and a swing set take stuffed animals on rides. Next to the swings, elves make gifts in Santa's Toy Shop. Santa himself pops out of a jack-in-the-box near the Ferris wheel. There's an airplane, too; its propeller spins and its wings rock as it comes in for a landing over a rooftop Nativity scene. The pilot, by the way, is Snoopy.

Perhaps the most grand Norton creation is his North Pole Express, a train that stands along the front of the display and is big enough to ride. Norton says, "It has smoke coming out of the smokestack and the cylinders. It has its separate sound system that plays a real steam engine sound and whistle! The wheels spin and the connecting arms function like a real locomotive. The circus car has several monkeys,

one of whom is spinning around in his basket." As if all of that weren't busy enough, strands of bulbs run everywhere in the Norton yard, from the lit archways leading into the display to the two giant NOELS on the roof to the gateposts wrapped to look like candy canes.

This happy electric madhouse takes weeks to set up and bumps up Norton's electric bill by more than $100. But he's used to it; he's been putting up the ever-growing spectacle since 1970.

One of the people who helps Norton set his display up is Keith LaPrath, a businessman in his twenties who lives down the block and wants to beat Norton at his own game. "We kind of play around with who can outdo the other each year," LaPrath has said.

They've been at it ever since LaPrath was a child, when the older man's displays inspired the kid to set up his own lights. In recent years, though, it's been LaPrath who's fired Norton up. "Keith's been the real inspiration for me to keep doing this. Just when I wonder if this might be the year to quit, he comes over, and I'm ready to do it again," Norton's admitted.

Like Norton, LaPrath has a train, a four-car job called the Christmas Express. The coal car carries toys and stuffed animals. In the box car, a bearded elf makes toys. The caboose has even more toys.

LaPrath's specialty, though, is stuffed animals. Reindeer (made by LaPrath's grandmother) drink coffee, presumably to stay warm. Two teddy bears pump an old-fashioned railroad handcar; another bear tries to light a lamp, even though the ladder under his feet keeps moving him away. Polar bears ride Santa's sleigh, a white reindeer in a Santa suit sits on a bridge and watches people go by, and rabbits put up a lamp in a miniature neighborhood.

Over everything, of course, are lights by the hundred. Icicle strands drip from LaPrath's rain gutters, lampposts stand guard throughout the display, and a web of lights leads up to a giant star standing several yards over LaPrath's roof. LaPrath says the setup is "like having a smaller version [of] Disneyland in your yard."

Iron Horses & Talking Cats

Certain things tend to show up a lot in displays for no particular reason. Trains, for instance. There's nothing especially Christmassy about industrial freight transport, wheezing engines, and squealing brakes. Carousels are another common sight. One can argue that carousels are not Christmassy at all. The proliferation of carousels makes one wonder whether lights displays are nothing more than a monument to nostalgia for one's carefree youth.

A very modern Christmas conceit is the presence of cartoon characters. But no one's yet been able to explain exactly how Sylvester the Cat's endless schemes to devour Tweety Bird line up with warm memories of families gathering around Old Tannenbaum.

The Lighting Bug

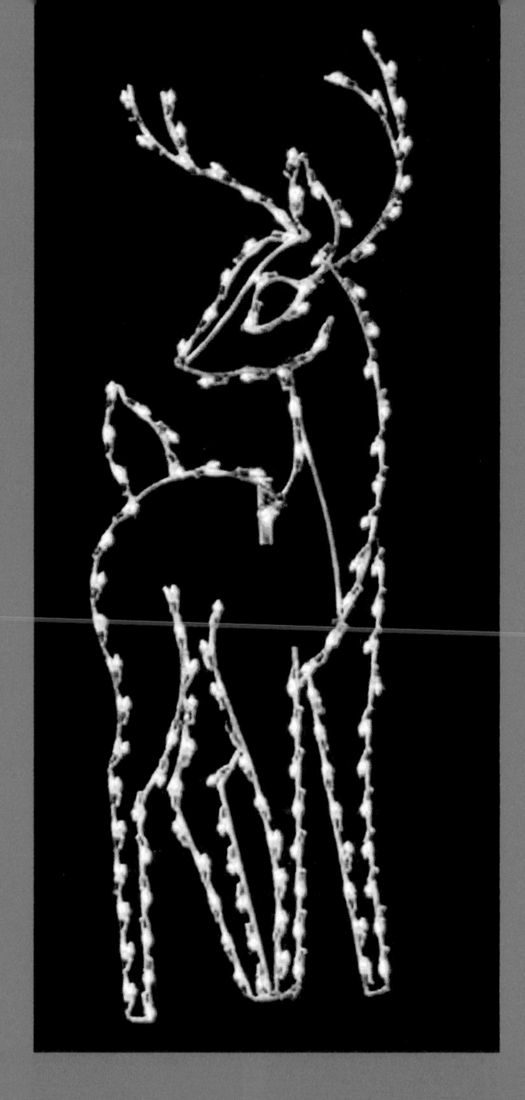

Putting up light displays is normal. But putting up jumbo extravaganzas is weird. Why do they get so big?

Time after time, the people who create the monsters say that they didn't start out intending to have a display that turned night into day. They began with a few strings of lights, then added a few more, then bought a wire-frame deer, then a family for the deer, and suddenly they found themselves investing in animated Santas and designing their own Dickensian scenes.

"It's almost like a disease, how much I keep decorating," Scott Elliott of Van Nuys, California, has said. The disease has apparently settled in for good. Elliott has decorated not just his own residence but his parents' home and their neighbors' as well.

The exact nature of the disease is hard to diagnose. New York houselighter Michael Korda (author of *Country Matters: The Pleasures and Tribulations of Moving from a Big City to an Old Country Farmhouse*) considers it physiological: "The problem, as I'm beginning to discover, is that this is addictive." Atlanta lighter Michael Albritton, taking a more psychological approach, has said, "I think it's creeping insanity." Richard Faucher, a helicopter builder who has covered his Delaware home with more than 600,000 lights, nailed down the exact psychosis, calling his display "a tribute to obsessive-compulsive behavior."

Among the symptoms is a glorious refusal to stop working when any sane person would. In late 1990, 76-year-old Kansas farmer Elmo Clark tore his shoulder and ended up with his arm in a sling as the lighting season approached. Nevertheless, he decorated his home with a display that attracted thousands of visitors, some coming from as far away as Australia and Yugoslavia.

Still, there's something more than sheer bullheaded mania at work. Richard Faucher of New Castle, Delaware, whose e-mail address starts with "iamsantac" and whose display includes 10-foot metal Christmas stockings he welded himself, sees his ever-growing, ever-changing display as an exercise in character: "If you don't challenge yourself, you lose your creativity." His wife, Linda, has seen it more in terms of public service: "There is more meaning than just lights. It's a place to come and it doesn't cost [the visitors] anything, but it brings people happiness."

Or to quote Scott Gluba of Aurora, Colorado, whose display has included Big Bird, Donald Duck, and gingerbread people, "It's all worth it when you see a kid smile or even an adult smile and say, 'Look at that.'"

Keeping Up with the Joneses

Norton and LaPrath are part of a trend. Like guys who compete over having a bigger backyard pool or a smaller-waisted wife, men all over the country try to out-light each other.

In Union City, California, the Teixeira and Peetz families of Clover Street have been amicably egging each other on for more than a decade. The neighbors' displays feature Santa Claus and his wife, a sleigh with reindeer, a rooftop snowman, a large manger scene, a Christmas tree covered in flashing red and green lights, wire-frame reindeer with moving heads and legs, and a fence lined with candy canes. Each year, the displays grow. The competition started in the early 1990s, when Dave and Yvette Peetz moved next door to the Teixeiras. The Peetzes installed a display that Christmas season. The next year, Dave and Tony Teixeira started "just clowning around" (as Tony's wife, Sally, puts it) with out-lighting each other, and the rivalry was on.

In Anchorage, Alaska, Tony Perez and Rob Loranger have been one-upping each another for less time but with more passion. Perez is said to have started it in 2002 when he bragged that he was going to get his home's picture on the front page of the *Anchorage Daily News* and, in an effort to do just that, put up more than 20,000 lights. In response, his buddy Loranger created a homemade Santa fishing from a pool of lights, another Santa and a Mrs. Claus in a motor home, a small-scale duplicate of the Loranger home, and a figure of Loranger himself putting up lights and getting an electric shock. Will the competition continue? Yes, says Perez; he is already planning his array for 2003.

In Orlando, Florida, Jay Miller and Andrew Santorelli have been fighting a friendly war of their own. Miller puts more than 15,000 lights on everything from his roof to three Christmas trees, a snowman, a star, angel figures, and a line of candy canes along his front walk. Santorelli keeps up handily, with thousands of lights and a number of animated figures. The two men started competing over lights years ago, and as Santorelli told the *Tampa Tribune,* "Every year since, I just wanted more."

That may be the motto of everyone who's trying to out-light his neighbor.

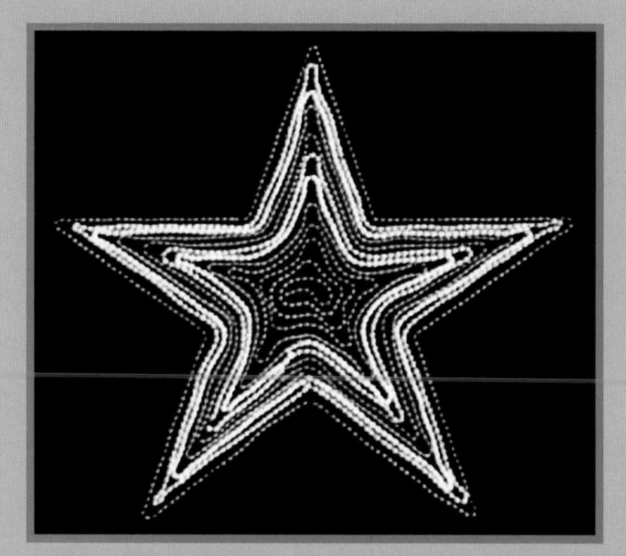

Lines of Lights

Want to make particular items stand out? Line them in rope lights, like these items from the home of Walter and Jackie Monkhouse in Alexandria, Louisiana.

Details, Details, Details

Elaborate displays like those of the Clot, Chartres, and Norton homes grab the eye with their wild complexity of figures and lights. But in some homes, one or two individual items stand out.

In the 37th Street neighborhood of Austin, Texas, one householder has strung lights so that they read, simply, FRED. Grant Nosbush of Eagan, Minnesota, has erected a small church that looks like a doghouse — or a doghouse that looks like a small church. The Aerts family of Monte Sereno, California, puts a flying saucer on the front lawn. Atop the roof of Joe Cavender of Federal Way, Washington, three spaceships approach a Mount Rainier made of lights, while in the yard stands a rendition of Seattle's Space Needle more than 20 feet tall.

Sculptures of lights are nice, but they're so art museum. Some lighters prefer effects straight out of a hard-rock concert. Not far from the Cavender home, Jerome and Sharilyn Drazkowski shine some of their nearly 30,000 lights at floating spheres produced by a bubble machine. In Woburn, Massachusetts, householder Bryce Gentry has erected a hologram projecting three-dimensional images of Christmas characters. In Minneapolis, Ron and Cathie Max set up an 8-foot-by-8-foot video screen to show dramatizations from the life of Christ.

Burglars, Beware!

Don't even think of robbing Travis Wetherington's home near New Bern, North Carolina. Santasaurus *(on the roof)* looks hungry.

A number of homes specialize in animals. Want to see a Tyrannosaurus Rex in a Santa hat? Bounce over to North Carolina and the Wetherington home, where a plywood-and-paint Santasaurus stands in full (though silent) cry on the roof. Enjoy insects? A pink ladybug, as tall as a living room, has hung on a stately home in Annapolis, Maryland, caught in mid-crawl up the front of the house. For those who thrill to turtles, Mike and Gwen Gaddy of Fayetteville, Georgia, erect a nine-foot Teenage Mutant Ninja Turtle doing a karate kick, courtesy of an auto windshield-wiper motor.

The most common item in home displays is Santa. Woodworking hobbyist Jeff Firnstahl has made and lit up a figure of Santa slam-dunking a basketball for his home in Andover, Minnesota. Santa rides a cow in Reseda, California, while he and Mrs. Claus play tennis on a real tennis court in Dalworthington Gardens, Texas.

But the most spectacular items have graced the spacious Maryland acreage of Earl Hargrove, Jr., who for decades has run a company specializing in big-time celebrations. Hargrove, Inc., has lit the National Christmas Tree since the Eisenhower days, created floats for rolling extravaganzas such as the Rose Parade in Pasadena, California, and prepared massive displays for events ranging from corporate trade shows to Miss America pageants, not to mention the occasional Olympic Games, Super Bowl, and World's Fair.

O Holy Night **Nativity scenes are also a common sight of the season. This one huddles on the roof of a Seattle home.**

A Hargrove Holiday

For more than 40 years, Earl Hargrove, Jr., lit up his Maryland home (pictured at right) with as many as 200,000 bulbs. He illuminated immense arches leading into the estate; a 20-foot cross; items specially made for the occasion, such as figures from Dr. Suess's *How the Grinch Stole Christmas*; and every window sill, door jamb, roof line, and other edge lining his two-story colonial mansion.

These items alone might account for the tens of thousands of spectators Hargrove has attracted each year — but there's more. Hargrove set some of his company's floats on his estate and lit them up, too. From Thanksgiving and Christmas parades came enormous snowmen, gift packages, and other signs of the season. One year, a giant Cabbage Patch doll married E.T., with an immense poodle conducting the ceremony. In 2001, as a sign of support to police and firefighters after the September 11 terror attacks, Hargrove added a full-sized fire truck and police car.

Good Night, Lights

Earl Hargrove has said that 2001 was his last year of lighting up his estate. All that remains are memories and photos.

Red, Light, and Blue

Like many other Americans, lights enthusiasts wanted to display the American flag at their homes after the terror attacks of September 11, 2001. For them, however, simply hanging up the flag wasn't enough. They plugged it in.

Many worked as big with their patriotic displays as they did with Santas and reindeer. Chuck Smith, king of the computer-driven PlanetChristmas, covered the roof of his house in an electrified flag. In Dix Hills, a town on Long Island, New York, 81-year-old Philippine immigrant Felipe Fider put up small-scale duplicates of the Statue of Liberty and the Twin Towers made from wood and plastic foam. In the Kansas City suburb of Raymore, Missouri, four neighbors decided to work together, covering all of their homes and the homes of other neighbors in lights of red, white, and blue. In Huntersville, North Carolina, homeowner Bob Confoy built an American flag 15 feet wide and covered it with about 40,000 lights; he told *The Charlotte Observer,* "It weighs a couple hundred pounds and took four of us to get on my garage."

The American flag has one special headache for lighters. How do you set up alternating rows of six and eight white stars on a tight blue rectangle without going bug-eyed from counting, checking, double-checking, and handling other mind-numbing details? John Sesso of Old Bridge, New Jersey — he of the $700 light bill and the 7-foot toy soldiers — solved the problem neatly. Instead of 50 tiny stars, he deployed a single big one.

Many if not most of these displays didn't reappear in 2002. It's a shame, really. Part of the fun of Christmas lights is in seeing the odd combinations of things: mangers next to penguins, Dickensian characters chockablock with cartoon characters, trains next to Santas, and American flags mixed with Christmas trees. After all, no one ever said that holiday lights had to make sense.

SEASON'S GREETINGS
GOD BLESS
AMERICA

Fields of White A flood of white lights adorns this Pennsylvania home. One might assume that it's a silent cry for snow.

Walls of Light

For all the wild conglomerations of objects, figures, and ephemera, there's nothing like simply slathering a building in bulbs. It's a style point, really. Some homes are as crowded with ornamentation as the palace of Versailles; others opt for the simplicity and power of the Pyramids.

Peter Reed is a pyramid builder. No Santas or snowmen will suit him, just tiny lights. Sixteen thousand of them, in red, pink, orange, green, and blue, turn the outside walls of his family's two-story home in Plaistow, New Hampshire, into glowing sheets. The bulbs don't stop at the walls; they run along the framework between the window panes and cover the handrails going up the steps to the front door. Nine thousand white lights blanket the trunk and branches of the tree in front of the house. In the past, Reed has left the roof dark, even though many other lights-mad houses bulb up their rooftops. But he plans to light up the roof the next time he does the house.

Powering the lights means stringing more than a thousand feet of extension cord. Five thousand staples keep the bulbs in place. Putting them in, a job that Reed shares with his girlfriend and her eleven-year-old daughter, is the easy part. The job that he dreads is pulling them out. The 10,000 holes they leave behind have caused his sister, Mary, who lives with him, to repaint the place.

The display pushes up his electric bill by more than $200. It'd be higher if he went with bigger bulbs, which is one reason why he uses tiny ones.

Most light fanatics put up their displays every year, but Reed prefers to do it every other year. He wants to keep the display a special event rather than something routine. Besides, his home attracts traffic jams of curious spectators, even in the daytime, and he wants to give a breather to his neighbors. And his sister. The spectators call out to the house's residents whenever they go out, he says, so "it's kind of embarrassing for her to walk from the car to the front of the house."

But then, Mary Reed isn't as enthusiastic about the lights as her brother is. "She thinks I'm nuts," he says.

What, Not Every Branch?

Peter Reed staples lights into nearly every slat of wood on the exterior of his home. Even the tree doesn't escape.

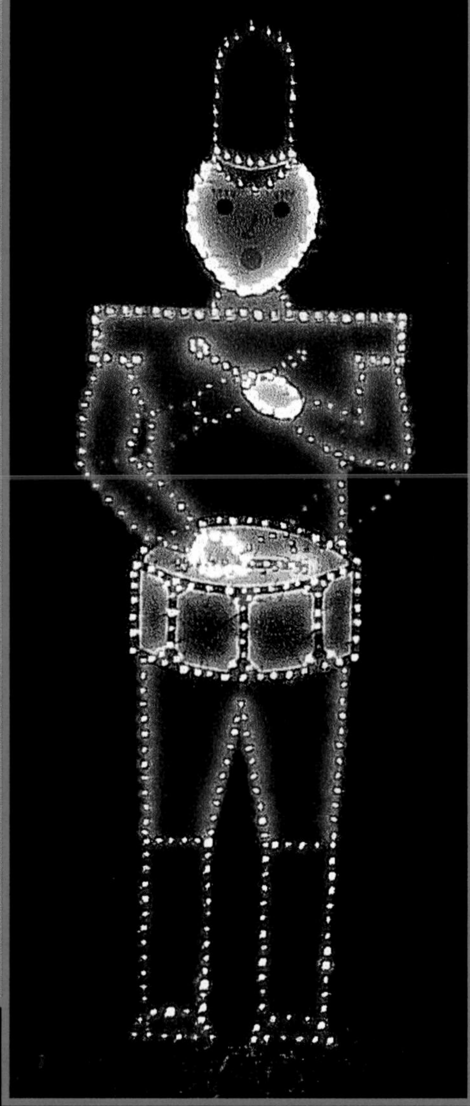

Move It

Above and at right: **Joe Faszl's poinsettias rise and bloom, his soldier bangs the drum, and his snowman dances. Walt Disney, you've got competition.** ***Below:*** **Thanks to computer-controlled animation, light sculptures of Santa and his reindeer can fly free into the night. Or seem to.**

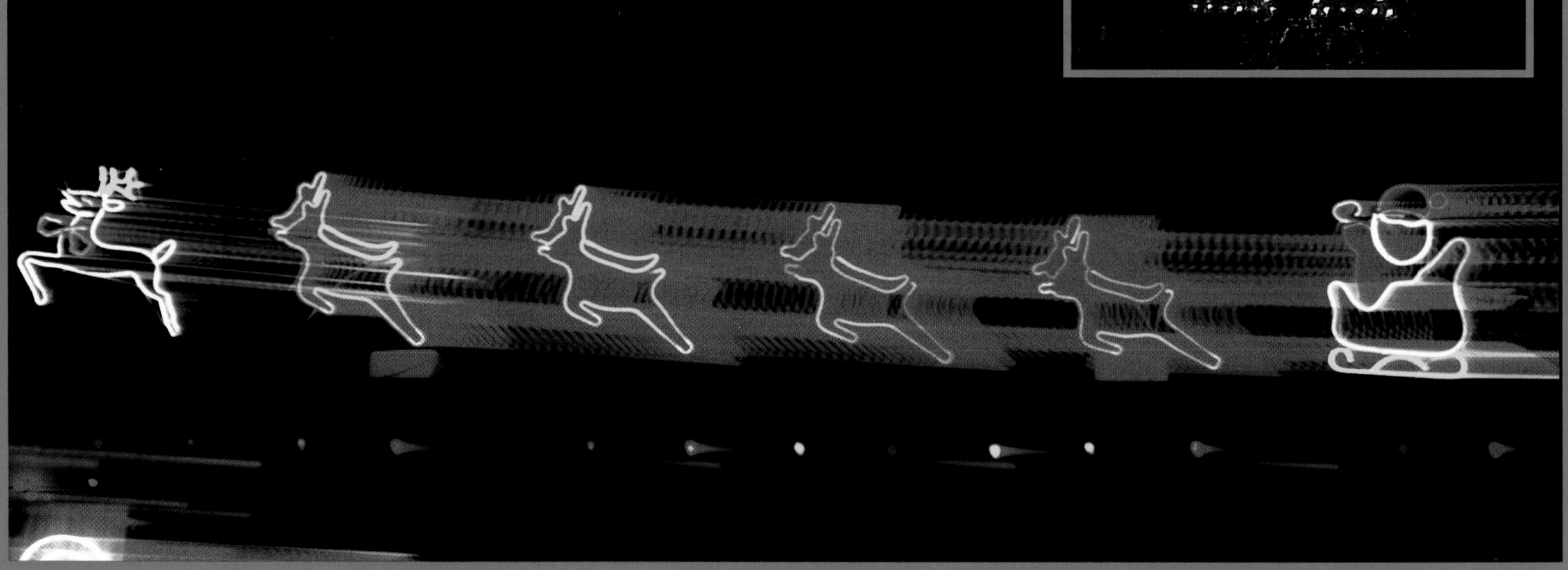

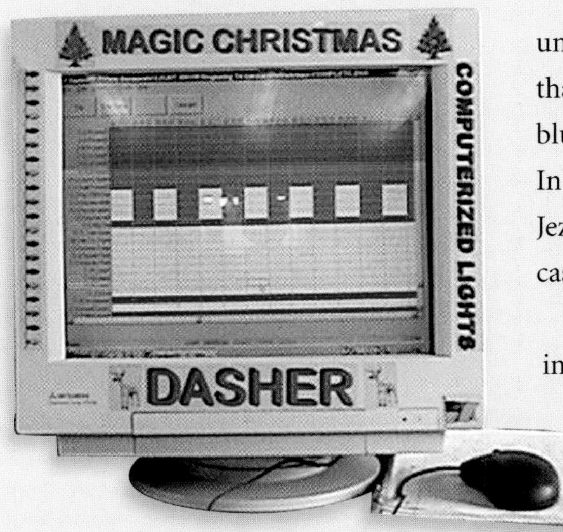

Computer Control

For decades, even centuries, scientists have dreamed of ways to get a variety of machines to work together smoothly. To create programs and software that allow a control panel in Houston to adjust the orbit of a space station 22,300 miles above the Atlantic Ocean, computer scientists have sweated rivers and burned ulcers into their guts. But leave it to home lighters to deploy this miraculously sophisticated, complex technology in order to make a wire-frame Rudolph's red nose flash on and off in time to "Grandma Got Run Over by a Reindeer."

Joe Faszl of Ballwin, Missouri, who calls his display Digital Christmas, has poinsettias made of lights that are set to turn on from the bottom up, making the flowers seem to grow and blossom. Cincinnati's Greg and Mary Hormann have a setup that counts down the number of seconds until Christmas, not to mention bushes that change color from red to green to blue and snowmen throwing snowballs. In Manassas, Virginia, Andy and Barbara Jezioro's setup has a webcam that broadcasts images of the display and its visitors.

At the home of Dan and Mary Baldwin in Garfield, New Jersey, seven Christmas trees stand proudly as their lights change color. Nutcracker soldiers rotate inside the turrets of a castle that is 7 feet tall and 14 feet wide. A whirligig that looks like a ceiling fan atop a four-legged stand turns around, taking passengers for a ride on its platform base.

But the champ of computer-controlled lights is Chuck Smith of Franklin, Tennessee, founder of PlanetChristmas.com. The only way to describe him is over the top — but in a good way. It's not just that he runs an Internet chat room and other resources for people who run computerized displays. The real reason is his home. Smith's 2002 display used almost 550 individual circuits and nearly eight miles of wire to control more than 130,000 tiny Christmas lights and 138 strobe lights. His carousel turns, his snowmen wave at visitors, his elves build a snowman, and his Santas pilot an airplane, ride a Harley, run a helicopter, water-ski with Rudolph, and play golf. (And, of course, he's got enough lit-up deer to form a luminous herd. Doesn't everyone?) The entire arrangement results in a show that runs more than 15 minutes and then starts all over again. (Unfortunately, Smith says that 2002 was the last year for this particular display. We hope that he'll find something else to do with all those wonderful lights.)

Smith says that his lights have shown up everywhere from *Oprah* to *The New York Times* to *Yahoo! Internet Life* magazine. His website, one of the most technically detailed in all of Christmas lightdom, includes schematics of his circuitry and photos of everything from electrical switching boxes and relays to the cables trailing out of the back of his computer. Unless you're an electrician, you've never seen so many cords, wires, cables, plugs, and power strips.

While equipment like this can cost thousands of dollars, there is one cost advantage. As the lights flash on and off, most of them are off at any given instant, so Smith's electric bills stay fairly reasonable. His massive display pushes his payments up by less than $60.

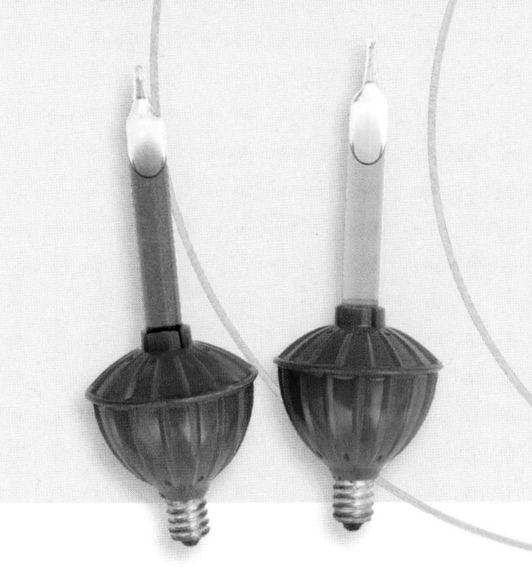

Mister Wizard

Drew Hickman is the Christmas lighters' Thomas Edison. He invented Dasher, the most famous Christmas-lights software program.

"It all got started, I guess, back when my brother and I were young lads," Hickman has said. "We got the idea that we could cut pumpkins out of wood, leaving holes in the shape of the eyes and the mouth. We then made a cardboard enclosure behind each of these holes and stuck a colored Christmas light into the container. They were the old, individual blinking kind, and the whole thing looked pretty neat, once all three lights started blinking randomly."

From there, Hickman was hooked on lights. In college, for instance, he and his brother (whom he roomed with) set up lights to form an angel that flapped its wings, using a switching system inspired by the turn signals in their father's 1964 Chevrolet Impala. Eventually, though, "I wanted an easier, faster, safer way to control things," Hickman says.

Since Drew had gone to college to study computer engineering, he spent much of the next few years designing a program that would use a PC's printer port to control Christmas lights. The result: Dasher.

Before everyone had a PC, lighting enthusiasts like Hickman used other machines to make their displays move, but the machines weren't flexible. Once the operator hooked one up to a part of his display, he could speed up or slow down the part's movements, but that was about it.

Computer control changed all that. From a home PC, a lights enthusiast can change the patterns and timing in which bulbs flash; set the times when the display turns on and off; program music to broadcast via loudspeakers or short-range radio; and even make the figures on the yard seem to react to each other. "Imagine having a display where you can change patterns on the fly," Hickman says. "Why not have a different pattern every night?"

Dash Away All

With the help of home computing, reels of wiring, and/or Hickman's Dasher program, home lighters can make figures dance, set trees of light to swirling, have lights chase each other up and down walls, and enact just about any other configuration of movement they can dream up.

Music, Music, Music

Quite a lot of homes use songs to enhance their lights. In the Minneapolis suburb of Plymouth, Tim and Cathy Fischer run an eclectic bunch of songs, including Mannheim Steamroller's high-tech, New-Age versions of "Stille Nacht" and "Hallelujah," "Please Come Home for Christmas" by light-metal Jersey boys Bon Jovi, Gene Autry's "Frosty the Snowman," and Sting's "I Saw Three Ships."

In Citrus Park, Florida, Joe Ayo turns his yard into a dance floor. He's played everything from George Michael's "Last Christmas" (remixed as a disco version) to Porky Pig singing Elvis Presley's "Blue Christmas" as lights flash in sync to the beat. Bouncing along with the music is a dancing Santa. Ayo pumps the songs through the displays on his lawn so that Nelly's "It's Getting Hot in Here (So Take Off All Your Clothes)" is sung by a snowman taking Nelly's part, with several reindeer doing the song's female lines.

Ayo's snowman is actually a robot — an animatronic automaton like the moving figures that populate Disneyland's Hall of Presidents or Pirates of the Caribbean — that Ayo has tricked up to look like the famous Frosty. "He will sing some songs, do some MC work between songs, and just enjoy the songs by staying somewhat alive during songs he is not a part of," Ayo has written on his website. "His mouth opens and closes, and [his] head turns. One arm has complete range of motion in shoulders, elbow, and wrists, and he can lean forwards or backwards a little." The result is dancing madness, bizarrely funky and funkily bizarre.

For extra dazzle and a bit of that dance-club atmosphere, Ayo has added to his display a smorgasbord of classic club light-up decor, including police car lights and rotating ball lights. In total, his display features some 40,000 individual bulbs. Like many other musical lighters, Ayo even has his own low-power, strictly local radio station; it blasts his tunes over any nearby radio tuned to 87.9 FM.

The Party Ain't Over

Eventually, even the most lights-mad householder thinks of quitting. As Chuck Smith of PlanetChristmas recently noted in a declaration of his intent to quit, "The older I get, the harder it is to get excited about going outside in 25-degree weather to put up Christmas lights."

Fortunately for fans of holidays, vernacular architecture, and happy wackiness, young lighters are learning to carry on the Good Weird tradition. Burbank's Keith LaPrath, as we've seen, started at age seven with a fairly small display, but after a few years, he was going toe-to-toe with the astounding Dick Norton. In Alberta, British Columbia, Doug Lawrence got his start at age twelve, inspired (like LaPrath) by a neighbor's setup. By the time he was seventeen, Lawrence was lighting up not just his own home but nearly his entire neighborhood.

And so the heritage of holiday lights rolls on. Young lighters take the place of their forebears with exuberance, impertinence, and no shame whatsoever, happily deaf to anyone who would accuse them of bad taste. Like the pioneering lighters who came before them, they compete with their neighbors, suck amperage from the local power grid, and make their home a jaw-dropping spectacle. Applying new technology to the same urges that drove earlier lighters, these young exhibitionists fill the air with garish neon colors, sentimental tunes, and limber sculptures that dip and dance courtesy of computerized motion control.

Ain't tradition grand?

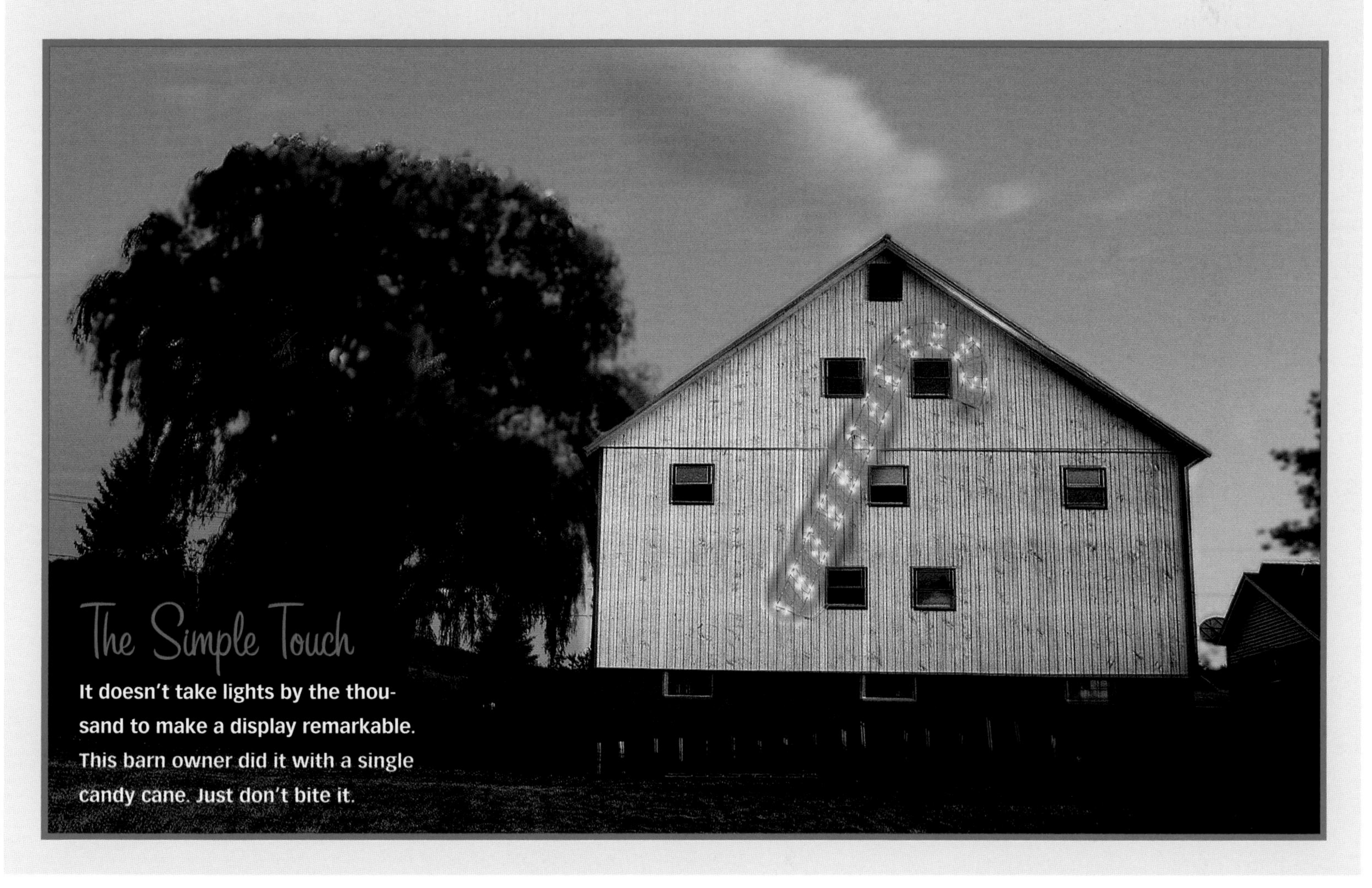

The Simple Touch

It doesn't take lights by the thousand to make a display remarkable. This barn owner did it with a single candy cane. Just don't bite it.

A Group Insanity

If you have a little time, a little money, and a few traits in common with Mad King Ludwig, you can pretty readily turn your home into a sizzling sunburst. But electrifying an entire neighborhood or town is a bigger job. It takes passion and ambition on the scale of Frank Lloyd Wright. It also requires a unique attitude toward conformity. People who turn entire communities into flashing sparkles are often good at working with others, while at the same time they deploy a happy disregard for anyone — yes, there are some Scrooges — who disapproves of them and their hobby.

Some snooty, high-brow-type people believe, or at least used to believe, that householders who shamelessly flaunt flashing lights, dazzling yard art, and screaming colors are vulgarians who don't realize the value of gentlemanly restraint. The truth is, these folks simply haven't gotten around much.

After all, it's mostly people approaching the upper slopes of the financial mountain who can afford to buy bulbs by the tens of thousands, computer-controlled switching systems, and, for the Nativity scene, hand-painted life-size sheep. Take the citizens of Saugus, a quiet and prosperous suburb, nearly 200 years old, north of that bastion of Yankee propriety, the city of Boston. Every year, the Saugus neighborhood of Lynn Fells Parkway blazes up. One house after another lines its windows and doorways with lights, wraps lights around trees, dangles lights from roofs, and plants Santas, snowmen, angels, and toy soldiers in the front yard. Compared to the homes of Dick Norton, Bill Clot, or Chuck Smith, each Lynn Fells home is pretty tame — but by old New England standards, the overall effect of the whole

neighborhood is as gaudy as Elvis in his rhinestone-jumpsuit era.

Another solidly respectable place that shimmers and sparkles in December is the Seattle neighborhood known as Ravenna, where the locals turn Park Road into Candy Cane Lane. Snowmen smile from inside windows, while a flat image of Santa and his reindeer hangs on a fence, with the lead reindeer flying off it. One home bears a sign with a drawing of a cute little dinosaur on wheels and the words TOY SHOP. Another house, with a sign over the front door reading SWEET SHOP, includes six-foot candy canes on the porch, hard candies in the windows, and giant lollipops stuck into the lawn like psychedelic daisies. Elves boost a figure in a Santa suit up the side of the house; he might be St. Nick himself, but

Welcome to Saugus

Four-year-old Anthony Devoe *(at left)* seems unimpressed by Saugus's lights. Saugusians turn a neighborhood street *(above)* into something like a covered bridge from times past — if times past had had electrified candy canes.

Candy Cane Lane

The homeowners of Seattle's Ravenna neighborhood *(above)* go all out — in a sensible, craftsmanlike, well-organized manner.

he has the green hands of the Grinch, or maybe Gumby. A team of four reindeer line up neatly atop a cornice, the first two leaping into the air and the other two placidly waiting their turn.

The star of the neighborhood is the carousel, a nearly full-size affair. It has horses, of course, but also a frog, rooster, ostrich, rabbit, ram, and camel. The animals are painted in a storybook style, mostly red and green (with brown and white accents, maybe to keep them from getting too tritely Christmassy). The beasts are, alas, just pictures, and no one can ride them, but they're nice to look at.

The locals say they've been lighting up Park Road and calling it Candy Cane Lane since 1949. Unlike a number of other private holiday light-ups, Candy Cane Lane doesn't accept donations to pay for the lights. The residents pull the cash from their own wallets. Any donations they receive go to the local food bank. And even though the most common question that visitors ask is, "Does everyone who moves in here sign a covenant guaranteeing that he'll light up his home?", the answer is no. It's all voluntary.

One might expect some wildness in a neighborhood self-proclaimed as Candy Cane Lane, but one would be disappointed. The Ravennans seem altogether sane and mature.

But not all neighborhoods can claim the same.

Guarding Brooklyn

With eyes so far apart that he can see in two directions at once, this toy soldier is no one to mess with.

Lights of the Heights

Brooklyn's Dyker Heights neighborhood is a comfortable, old-fashioned Italian-American community of single-family homes and quiet, safe streets. But on winter nights, the place explodes. More than 100,000 people from as far off as Japan visit each year to see the Dyker Heights holiday lights displays, such as the tree covered in lights, with colored balls that hang like electric fruit; the snowman holding a broom with fiber-optic bristles; and the reindeer posed nobly between two marble lions flanking a front stoop.

The most elaborate creations, though, aren't just collections of light bulbs. They're concepts. There's a Small World home, for instance, with (among other things) a rotating globe; national symbols from around the world, like a Dutch windmill and a Leaning Tower of Pisa; and a moving Ferris wheel ridden by dolls. In fact, passersby will encounter dolls and other little figures all over the place. The effect is at once awe-inspiring, cute, and a little eerie.

Dyker Heights householder Michael Caso — a fan of *A Christmas Carol* and *Scrooge,* a 1970 movie musical with Alfred Finney as Scrooge and Alec Guinness as Marley — has set up illuminated figures of the film's characters, about thirty of them, full-sized and properly costumed and posed. Through loudspeakers, Caso has poured the *Scrooge* soundtrack, which includes Scrooge's song "I Hate People" and Marley's "See the Phantoms" ("If you think life is miserable now . . . / The next world / Is far, far worse!"). Ho ho ho.

A block away, Lucy and Angelo Spata have erected arches, spiral Christmas trees, and miniature villages, not to mention snowflakes the size of linebackers. However, the arrangement that anchors the Spata display is often musical. Dozens of angels, arranged in a wide semi-circle and lit from within, blow long trumpets as they guard the Spatas' property. An entire life-size boys' choir has stood there, too, frozen in mid-hymn and looking as pious as only plastic blow-molds can.

But the true champ of Dyker Heights is Alfred Polizzotto, a real estate lawyer. Pollizzotto set up his first lights display in celebration of his recovery from cancer, and it's his example that others in

Brooklyn Fever

No angel lacks for company at the Spata home *(at right)*. And in Brooklyn, even reindeer *(below)* stand tough. When they guard a Tannenbaum, no one gets near it.

Horsing Around **At the Polizzotto home, a soldier horses around while others (and a batch of reindeer) watch for trouble.**

the neighborhood have followed. With its balconies and two-story columns, Polizzotto's Greek Revival mansion would look at home on an antebellum plantation, but his Christmas décor is strictly Goliath Modern.

Before the Polizzotto columns stand two Nutcracker-type toy soldiers, each more than 25 feet tall. Immense white horses rear up, nearly throwing their riders. On the balcony, a line of serious-faced reindeer watch over the entire show. In the middle of it all, just a few feet before the front door, stands a Santa Claus easily twice as tall as any of the visitors to the display. With his outstretched arms reaching toward the crowd, and his mouth a half-moon grin of almost excessive glee, Santa seems to be welcoming guests into either a cozy workshop or a bubbling, carnivorous stewpot. One can almost imagine Santa saying, "Fredo, paisan, lemme hug ya! What's this I hear about ya weaslin' on the Family?"

The Light Police

Not every neighborhood loves its holiday lights.

In some places, the objection is aesthetic. When city laborers began hanging white lights on the trees of Boston's distinguished Commonwealth Avenue in 1999, a number of neighborhood residents objected. The chairman of the neighborhood association complained that the arrays' electrical conduits "look like the contractor just threw up whatever he had in the truck." Others griped that the city was "cheapening" and "tarting up" the neighborhood and insulted residents who liked the lights. At least 300 signed a petition asking the city to take the lights down. Nevertheless, the city went ahead as planned, and the lights went on.

In Pecan Grove, Texas, a homeowners association told local lights king Steve Richardson to dim his display, or else they'd get an injunction against him. They found his bubble machine to be especially objectionable. But Richardson stood up for his soapy little spheres, and the machine bubbled on.

Sometimes, the problem isn't so much aesthetic as cultural, especially in the British Isles. "Here in the city of Dickens' *A Christmas Carol*, signs of the season are, outside of a few major shopping streets, tough to find," wrote *Fortune* magazine correspondent Justin Fox in 2001. When a transplanted American put up lights outside his home in the London neighborhood of Chiswick, his neighbors asked him to take them down. "Four-foot-tall plastic Santa Claus puppets have no place in Chiswick front gardens — except in a dust bin," one neighbor e-mailed.

The objections aren't limited to London. In Irvine, an industrial waterfront town in Scotland, the residents of the Wardlaw Gardens neighborhood got a court order to stop David Rowlands from lighting up his 8,500-bulb display at night. Afternoon lightings were permitted, although burning outside lights in the daytime is usually a pointless exercise. Speaking for Kilmarnock Sheriff Court, which issued the judgment, Sheriff David Smith said that Rowlands had created a nuisance "substantial and more than is tolerable in a quiet, peaceful location."

The danger of fire is another main thrust behind the anti-light urge. In 2001, for example, Pennsylvania State University officials ordered dormitory residents to take down the lights they'd hung on the dorm's exterior walls, for fear that some trees nearby would catch fire.

Then there's religion. In 2000, when parents of Christian students at Mariners Elementary School in Newport Beach, California, put up Christmas lights on the school, parents of Jewish children complained. A local rabbi, Mark Miller of Temple Bat Yahm, called placing the lights on a public building "a provocative act." The people who put them up said they weren't trying to provoke anything except a few smiles. Still, the lights came down.

BUILDING

Awestruck

A young boy revels in the lights of the Pedernales Electric Company's display in Johnson City, Texas.

Come Here, Children

Not all holiday displays stick with the Santa-and-reindeer theme. In these Austin displays, Jack Skellington seems ready for Austin's kids to sit in his lap and ask for presents. Nearby, Elvis, Marilyn, and some longhorns await Santa.

James Brown Lives **Willis Littlefield of Austin, Texas, sets his animated Santas dancing to the groove of James Brown. If visitors look closely, they'll see that one of these dancing fools is James Brown himself.**

From Little Nuts . . .

How do neighborhood-wide riots of light get started? Sometimes, a single person can make it happen. One of the country's biggest displays, the 37th Street neighborhood in Austin, Texas, began with one resident, a cheery eccentric named Jamie Lipman. "I just started putting up Christmas lights [about 15 or 16 years ago]," Lipman told CNN. "Nothing exotic, but it grew a little bit year in, year out." One year, Lipman and Bob Godbout, a neighbor who lives across the street, decided to string lights between their homes. "Once we did that, everybody said, 'Wow, we wanna do that.'" Eventually, the entire street lit up and became an attraction that now draws eager spectators from all over central Texas and beyond.

Sometimes group displays grow from competition. Scientists may say that electricity powers the lights in Windward Pointe, a neighborhood of the prettily named small town Holly Springs, North Carolina. The scientists are wrong. Something a little hotter strikes the sparks. "What was supposed to be a fun little neighborhood decorating contest has turned into a 'no lights barred Griswold Family Christmas,'" according to Holly Springs resident Charles Dickson. (The Griswolds are the film family of *National Lampoon's Christmas Vacation,* in which father Clark goes overboard with lights.)

As the *Raleigh News and Observer* reported in 2002, "At night they [the Holly Springs residents] sneak around switching out bulbs to make someone's Frosty turn blue [and] adding naughty letters to someone's 'Ho, ho, ho.'" It's all in a spirit of friendly fun and playing games . . . in the way that pro football, which kills collarbones and breaks ribs, is a game. "We sit and stare at each other," Windward Pointer Patrick Anderson has said. "Then we run out and get more lights."

The result: a neighborhood that year after year has lit up almost every outside surface and overpopulated its lawns with illuminated animals. The competition is amicable — at least so far.

One Man, Many Lights

Sometimes, people just don't cooperate. You might want your entire neighborhood to shine like a hundred constellations, but the folks next door and across the street don't have your enthusiasm. What to do?

Paul Damon and John Shea found an answer. Damon lives in Diamond Lakes, the Minneapolis neighborhood where he grew up, and takes it on himself to cover it in hundreds of thousands of lights. A serious Christian — "the more I learned to honor Christ, the more [the lighting]'s meant to me" — he says that he gets his design ideas through prayer. Naturally, they're religious in nature (Nativity scenes, for instance), and the star of his setup is a cross standing 100 feet off the ground, covered in more than 4,000 lights. Like a virtuoso musician who generally plays solo but sometimes conducts, Damon has gotten help with the design and construction of some of his exhibits, but he's clearly the man who makes it all happen.

Shea, an energetic elementary school teacher in Juno Beach, Florida, is another who both plays his own instrument and leads the band. He lights his home thoroughly enough, with a good 20,000 bulbs. In 2000, though, he decided to decorate his neighborhood. As neighbor Teresa Eskew said, "He rented a lift. He just went up and down the street one Saturday, with a big, big string of lights, and put them on people's houses."

"I made a deal with the neighbors," Shea explained. "I provide the lights, and you provide the power." He did a good job, too. "You'd [have] thought he was a pro," Eskew said. He did more than just string lights. "We ran sixty 30-inch-tall trumpet-playing angels all the way up the street," Shea remembered. "It turned into a community effort. Everyone pitched in."

And that suited Shea just fine. "He just thinks everybody should get into the spirit," Eskew said. "He has a little radio station, a kit, you can only hear it on our street, and everybody has recorded messages. He's just like that."

The King of Lights

One man. One house. Six hundred thousand little lights. Introducing Rich Faucher of New Castle, Delaware.

No Lingering Lights Allowed

Even neighborhoods that tolerate lavish and/or garish light displays sometimes have a limit: time.

Chicago Sun-Times columnist Mark Brown noted thirty-five homes burning lights in his neighborhood during late January, 2003. "What seems to be developing is that the white lights have become more of a 'winter decoration' that is bleeding across the calendar," he wrote. "This started, of course, with the stores and merchandisers who kept moving up the holiday shopping season until the rush now begins on the day after Halloween . . . What was once a delightful novelty is becoming boring electric clutter."

Brown isn't the only one to call publicly for a seasonal end to lights. "Memo to my neighbor: Yes, those new dangling icicle things were beautiful in December, but soon they will look ridiculous," Boston journalist Diane Daniel wrote in early 1999. "There should be a law: No holiday lights, wreaths, ribbons or ornaments of any kind shall be visible to the public after January 15."

Actually, there are such laws. In 2002, inspectors for the city of Biddeford, Maine, came into local restaurants and ordered them to take their lights down. After all, it was April, and a city lighting regulation allowed strings of lights for periods "not to exceed 45 days." The reason for the regulation was safety, based on the theory that exposure to weather could cause so much wear on the lights that pumping electricity through them would create a fire hazard. But when the merchants complained, the mayor and other local politicians said that they'd consider rescinding the decades-old law.

Creepy Crawlies

Bob Gould's Kansas City neighborhood makes webs that Spiderman himself would envy. Here, visitors get a pondside view — *or perhaps* they're neighborhood residents, escaping the crowds of sightseers that come to *ooh* and *aah.*

Light Flight **If you can't beat 'em, join 'em. Thanks to the wonders of modern photography, individual lights can become bright streamers, reminiscent of those in the Gould neigborhood. It makes for a great holiday postcard.**

The Architect's Holiday

As an architect, Bob Gould understands design and the use of space. As a holiday lighter, he understands the value of tossing strings of bulbs at random. That's more or less what he did one year in the mid-'90s, flinging lights from tree to tree in his yard.

Initially, his neighbors in Kansas City, Missouri, didn't much like the spider-webby look that Gould's lines of lights produced as they criss-crossed over one another. But the web eventually caught them. By 2000, the neighbors were joining Gould, hurling vines of light from treetop to treetop. The stronger of them threw the lights entirely over the trees. With its ends touching the ground and the midpoint suspended midair, each glowing rope formed a peak that looked like the outline of a circus tent. Other lights banked off the ground at sharp angles like laser beams or dipped in soft, lazy curls that grazed the grass and put a diffused glow on the surface of a nearby pond.

Visitors don't just look at the lights and walk past them, as they do with other displays. They walk among the strands, stepping over some and ducking under others as even more light lines dip nearby, like the paths of planes dropping in for a landing. "The lights create an ethereal atmosphere," Gould said. "The tunnels and peaks of light envelop you. They change the scale of the neighborhood and become a surprising sculptural object."

Gould has rigged up a simple way to make a lights web: Connect a baseball to some twine, toss the baseball over a tree, tie a strand of lights to the twine, and pull on the baseball. If you've done it right, you'll pull the lights straight into the tree.

But Gould isn't fussy about means and methods. "It's all guesswork," he told *Southern Living* magazine. "Our philosophy is 'What's done is right.' A neighbor will throw up a strand and say 'What do you think?', and I will reply, 'Well, it's up there; I like it!'"

Real Traffic Stoppers

The most common objection among neighborhoods with lighted homes is traffic. A well-lit neighborhood will attract throngs of spectators, most of them encased in the comfort of their automobiles. The slowly moving cars form long rows that block residents from getting home. Sometimes sightseers even park on neighbors' property. In Monte Sereno, California, the neighbors of the Aertses — the family with a flying saucer in the yard — asked the city to limit outdoor displays for Christmas and Halloween. (The Aertses put up big displays for Halloween as well as Christmas.) "This is just one notch away from the community that banned American flags," Alan Aerts shot back.

Not everyone fights so hard. For more than 20 years, Ted and Kim

Kresge of St. Petersburg, Florida, set up a display that put the evening stars to shame. But in 2001, the neighbors got fed up with the tens of thousands of cars full of people coming to see the Kresges' tens of thousands of lights. The neighbors threatened a lawsuit, and the Kresges caved. "We've reduced [the display] by about 90 percent," Ted Kresge said at the time. "It's still pretty, but it's nothing like it was." Though he sounded resigned to the dim-down, he allowed himself to fire a final shot: "We were trying to say peace and goodwill to men, but there wasn't any peace."

A similar case hit Bob and Sandy Kendall of Chanhassen, Minnesota. They agreed to turn off their five-year-old display, which included animal figures and a musical carousel, when the city council outlawed it. The council, responding to neighborhood complaints, passed a resolution telling the Kendalls to obey all city laws on parking, noise, and excessive lighting. The mayor said, "We appreciate the effort and contribution you make to Christmas. [The resolution] is not our attempt to put a burden on you." One doubts that the Kendalls saw it that way.

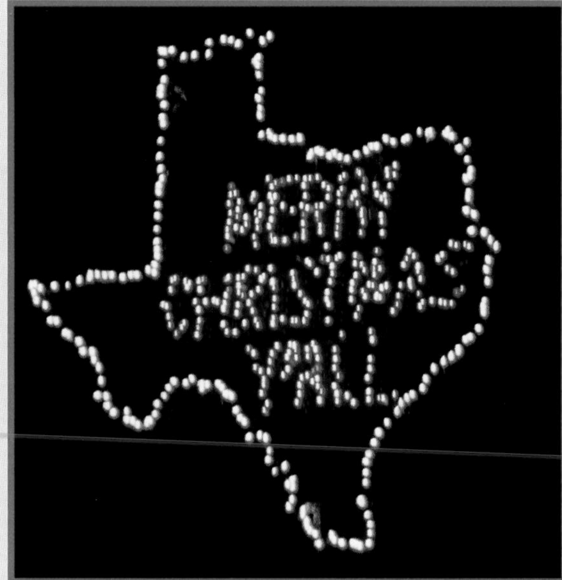

Holiday lighting fanatics in Austin offer passing sightseers a wide range of visual delights *(this and facing page)*. Though different in arrangement, they are all equally representative of true Texas style — wired for maximum luminosity and almost frighteningly cheerful.

God Blessed Texas

Texas, it's said, is like a whole other country. It's also said that they do things big in Texas. Nowhere are those clichés more true than in the parade of the state's lit-up neighborhoods.

Austin alone has more than one neighborhood populated by galaxy-class light maniacs. The 37th Street area, sometimes called — always with great fondness — the Lightmare on 37th Street, has included a rotating lights display on an oak tree, a futuristic tower of light strands still packaged in their boxes, a Volkswagen lit up inside and out, a menorah made out of liquor bottles, a giant peace sign, columns wrapped in red and white lights to look like enormous candy canes, and endless strands of bright white lights roving across streets, between homes, and from tree to tree. The more irreverent of the locals have tied Barney the dinosaur (that great purple behemoth beloved of children and anathema to adults) to railroad tracks, and they've talked of putting an effigy of Osama bin Laden in a Santa suit. If displaying holiday lights is a sign of individual expression, then the individuals of 37th Street are mad poets, the Hieronymus Bosches of holiday lights.

Psychedelic **Visitors stop to admire the famous Trail of Lights in Zilker Park.**

Their closest competition comes from Austin's Zilker Park neighborhood. The displays aren't quite as weird as those of 37th Street, but they're every bit as extensive and elaborate. You enter the Zilker Park Trail of Lights through a long, curving, multicolored tunnel of bulbs that is wide enough for a dozen people to pass through shoulder to shoulder. Beyond the tunnel, you find the Cat in the Hat, the Twelve Days of Christmas, children's drawings, and a canopy of stars. The setup has also included a globe with, for some reason, dolphins circling it as if they were swimming in midair. But the star of the show is a cone of light strands that forms a Christmas tree more than 150 feet tall. You can see it for miles. Some people — children, of course, but also some adventurous adults — enjoy getting inside the thing, spinning around until they're dizzy, and then falling on the ground face up to watch the lights swirl around.

Almost as famous as Austin's Zilker Park and 37th Street is the Arlington neighborhood of Interlochen. Its displays aren't as wild as those in Austin, but it makes up for the difference handily. For one thing, Interlochen's a venerable veteran in the lights game; it's been shining for about a quarter of a century. It's also one of the bigger lit-up 'hoods: The total of illuminated homes in the area has topped two hundred. And in addition to the thousands of bright bulbs, the neighborhood has offered carolers, brass bands, and other entertainments. A local airline even offers airborne tours of Interlochen and other electric areas in Arlington. The neighborhood is so popular that the cops make special arrangements to help the residents cut through the hundreds of visiting drivers who come night after night to gawk. The police block off some streets, and allow only the cars with special, residents-only tags to enter them and get home.

Other Texas neighborhoods specialize. The people of University Hills in Irving don't just turn on lights; they've become part of their displays by dressing up as the three Wise Men and other members of the traditional Nativity scene. Meanwhile, Plano's Deerfield neighborhood includes more deer than the cast of *Bambi.* In the Springpark section of Garland, neighbors have worked together to create, among other things, the entire village of Whoville from *How the Grinch Stole Christmas.*

But none of these areas can beat Marble Falls, where it seems that the whole town collaborates to delight and possibly blind any visitors. The result is the Christmas Walkway of Lights. Visitors pass through a lit-up tunnel and stroll past display after display, but the real prize is Lake Marble Falls. The golden reflection of the city's million-plus lights on the water can be so stunning that a spectator may find himself staring transfixed at the sight until icicles start dangling from his nose.

Mysteries and Scandals

Holiday lights are fairly benign items, but occasionally they get connected to stuff that's inexplicable or even criminal.

For almost thirty years, someone has removed two of Anchorage innkeeper Sue Hahn's many red bulbs, and substituted a blue bulb and a green one. Whoever it was later began leaving Christmas ornaments, too, and cards signed "B and G" (for "Blue and Green"). No one has ever discovered the bulb-swapper's identity.

In 2002, carnival operator Ed Gregory of Tennessee filed for bankruptcy so that he could avoid paying the millions of dollars that he owed his creditors. Nevertheless, he lit up his home that Christmas with thousands of lights in a display "described by some as a mini-Opryland [amusement park]," said investigative reporter Phil Williams of nearby Nashville's WTVF television. A lawyer for one of the creditors commented, "I find it amazing that the Gregorys can find the money to fund this holiday lighting and still, at the same time, inform their secured creditors that they might not be able to make the . . . payment on their home this month." Williams added, "Ed Gregory tells me his family just didn't want to give up their annual holiday tradition, and he's paying for the display out of the income he's received since filing for bankruptcy. But his creditors are arguing that if he really is bankrupt, he should at least look like it."

Just a Small Town

Despite its diminutive size, Gatlinburg, Tennessee, offers a light show of grand decadence, including light-drenched homes *(below),* chaotic parades *(inset),* annual fireworks, and, of course, the traditional hayride that brings visitors around to see all these sights.

City Lights

With Marble Falls, we leave the domain of householders and go into government and politics. For even wilder than lit-up neighborhoods are the whole municipalities that go mad for lights.

With fewer than 4,000 residents but more than 25,000 visitors a day (on average), the Tennessee hamlet of Gatlinburg lives to attract tourists. It lies near the tourist destinations Dollywood and Great Smoky Mountains National Park, but one of its biggest attractions is Winterfest.

Winterfest is an annual eight-million-light event that Gatlinburg shares with the nearby communities of Pigeon Forge and Sevierville. Running from November up through February, it's not solely a Christmas celebration. According to George Hawkins, the special events manager of the Gatlinburg Department of Tourism, "It has brought people in who are looking for something to do at a time there's normally not anything going on."

Gatlinburg does not disappoint. Almost all of the local businesses get slathered in lights, as do the trees along the nearby Little Pigeon River. The town also offers a Fantasy of Lights Christmas Parade and tours of the local lights by trolley and hay wagon. In a touch more suited to the Fourth of July than the dead of winter, Winterfest's kickoff night includes fireworks and a chili cookoff.

The event itself is not unusual (well, not terribly unusual), but the level of organization is. Gatlinburg takes its lights seriously. In 2000, the city brought in a lighting design company to ensure that the local businesses, especially the ones near the Little Pigeon, fit the town's standards. "It is important to decorate with a look that is appropriate for the entire season of winter — with lights, greenery, ribbons, bows, and snowflakes," says the application for the town's Official Illumination and Decoration Contest, which runs competitions in categories that include Best Window Display, Best Retail/Shop, Best Mall, Best Restaurant (Large), and Best Restaurant (Small). "Colored lights are acceptable when appropriate; however, WHITE LIGHTS are emphasized."

Santa, Stop Here!

Neighboring rowhouses in Baltimore, Maryland, are decorated in blinding style, with reindeer (and their elf keepers) on the roof to show Santa the way.

The Grid That Stole Christmas

The year 2000 saw a new line of opposition to holiday lighters: an electricity shortage.

In that year, California suffered an energy crisis. Blackouts and brownouts rolled across a number of its cities. Even in places where the lights stayed on, rates shot up as if they'd been bounced off a trampoline. State and local governments encouraged citizens to cut down their use of electricity.

By December, the governments were aiming their concerns at holiday lighters, asking them to put up fewer holiday lights than usual and to fire up their displays for shorter periods. The California Independent System Operator, which runs a power grid for much of western United States, noted that the electricity that California's holiday lights eat up could power at least a million homes without holiday lights. Grim references to "the grid that stole Christmas" began circulating.

Cities and amusement parks that planned big light shows canceled them or toned them down. Less than an hour after Governor Gray Davis turned on the lights for the state's official Christmas tree, he turned them off.

Neighborhoods of holiday lighters felt the pressure. While some dimmed down considerably, they didn't like doing it. "[P]eople . . . count on these lights being on. We collected nine tons of food and $6,000 cash for the needy in our [donation] barrels last year," said Dick Martin, a householder in the Sacramento neighborhood of Orangevale's Dovewood Court, which in earlier years had lit up like a magnesium flare. The people of San Jose's light-filled Willow Glen area cut back — but only a little. Resident Susan Walton explained, "Doing the lights is a welcome full of peace and joy and happiness."

While some of California's lighters continued to blaze, the worry about electricity shortages spread to other states, especially those on the same power grid as California. Officials in Washington, Oregon, and Utah asked citizens to cut back.

Even outside the western power grid, holiday lighters and others began to worry so much about their own electricity supply that public officials felt the need to head off a full-scale panic. "The California Power Crisis: Can It Happen in Pennsylvania?" asked Douglas Biden of Pennsylvania's Electric Power Generation Association in a press release; his answer was no. In Texas, state senator David Sibley and state representative Steven Wolens put out an announcement titled "Why the Grinch Won't Steal Christmas in Texas" in an effort to reassure citizens.

By the 2001 holidays, thankfully, California's energy crisis had apparently vanished, and so had the governments' concerns about the wattage of holiday lights. Or as California Energy Commission spokeswoman Susanne Garfield said, "After the year that [California] has had, go ahead. Merry Christmas."

A Summer Place

For six months of the year, McAdenville, North Carolina, is a nondescript hamlet dominated by the Pharr Yarns textile mill. Nothing much happens there; as former mayor Bill Miller (a Pharr Yarns employee) has said, "When you run [for office] here, you don't run on issues."

But starting in summer, this village of fewer than 900 people begins turning into Christmastown. The nickname appears on the postmark stamped on Christmas cards mailed from there, on the sign welcoming visitors at the city limits, and in just about everything written about the town since 1956.

In that year, the local Men's Club started lighting the town for Christmas. The event was nothing big at first, featuring just the nine trees around the local community center. But with Pharr Yarns's help — just about nothing happens in McAdenville without Pharr Yarns — the tradition expanded.

Santa, Santa

One should never believe the rumors that Santa does not exist. Look here — at this McAdenville building (*below*), he's hanging out with Frosty.

These days, more than 400,000 lights cover McAdenville. The job of putting them in place is so big that it begins in August, when North Carolina's humidity and heat would make any ordinary person move as little as possible. Pharr Yarns pays McAdenvillers to check each bulb for breakage or burnout and then start stringing up the lights.

Virtually all of the town's nearly 400 trees get the treatment, with each one being decorated with at least 500 lights — and some getting more than 5,000. Especially picturesque are the trees that line a local lake. Like the lights of Marble Falls, the glow of McAdenville's lights on the water exerts a draw for photographers that only a nude movie star could match.

The town depends on more than just trees for its visual thrills. It has a lighted fountain in the center of the lake, a display

Bedazzlement

In McAdenville, street lights are hardly necessary during the holiday season. Sheer candlepower can hold spectators spellbound *(top)*. And cars drive between rows of giants *(inset)*.

of Santa plus reindeer that runs more than 70 feet, and a lighted image of Old Man Winter, nearly 50 feet long, blowing snowflakes through the sky. Individual householders join in with such setups as gingerbread people in mid-dance around a gingerbread house complete with candy-cane fences.

The glow from McAdenville pulls visitors from as far off as Atlanta, more than 200 miles away. Church groups arrange bus tours of the lights, and the Carolinas Miata Club and Carolina Z Club (for fans of Datsun Z model cars) organize drives to enjoy them — with the top down, of course. The lights' beauty reportedly inspired bride Wendy Abernathy to get married there in 2001. The mere name of the town has become something of a touchstone. "If you could harness the energy of UNC-Charlotte's new women's basketball coach," wrote journalist Susan Shackelford in 2001, "you could power the McAdenville holiday lights."

And so it goes. Nothing seems able to stop the McAdenville lights, not even when Pharr Yarns started selling its property and turning over its long-held responsibilities, like supplying the town's electricity, to the local government in late 2002. As commentator Dave Baity reported, "The company will continue paying for [the lights]. That's good to hear. Turning out the lights that attract hundreds of thousands each December would be a tragic loss."

Bits & Pieces

A few neighborhoods do stuff that is distinctive even by the cheerfully eccentric standards of other well-lit neighborhoods.

Sometimes, the distinction is sheer candle power. Roselle, Illinois, lies not very far from Chicago O'Hare International Airport. The displays on Roselle's May Street get so bright that they've caught the attention of flight crews soaring in and out of O'Hare. Fortunately, they have not yet proved a hazard to aviation.

Elsewhere, a single item stands out. For sheer size, few individual items can beat a sleigh more than 20 feet long, holding reins that stretch nearly 200 feet, across the length of three houses before they reach the reindeer — not to mention the 33-foot snowman nearby. They're set up for Randy Brusse, who lived in Farmington, Minnesota. He and his neighbors were sitting around, talking about outdoing another neighbor who had erected a big star, but no one did anything until after Brusse died in 1998. Brusse's widow, Lisa, and his neighbors Chuck Isenmann and Doug and Jessica Peterson teamed up to erect these giants as a tribute to Randy.

But for superb cooperation, not to mention overcoming ugly odds, the crown goes to a community in the San Francisco Bay area. The east side of Oakland, California, is a rough area that gets dozens of homicides per year — except on Picardy Drive between Seminary and 55th Avenues. The residents of this mixed-race, middle-class neighborhood, known for towered Tudor-style buildings straight out of Elizabethan England, have banded together to make the place safe and attractive. Part of that effort is the strands of lights that they run from house to house, literally connecting every home on the street, a tradition that's been building up for decades. They may not always agree on how to pronounce the street's name — *PIC*ardy or Pi*CAR*dy? — but they all like the lights.

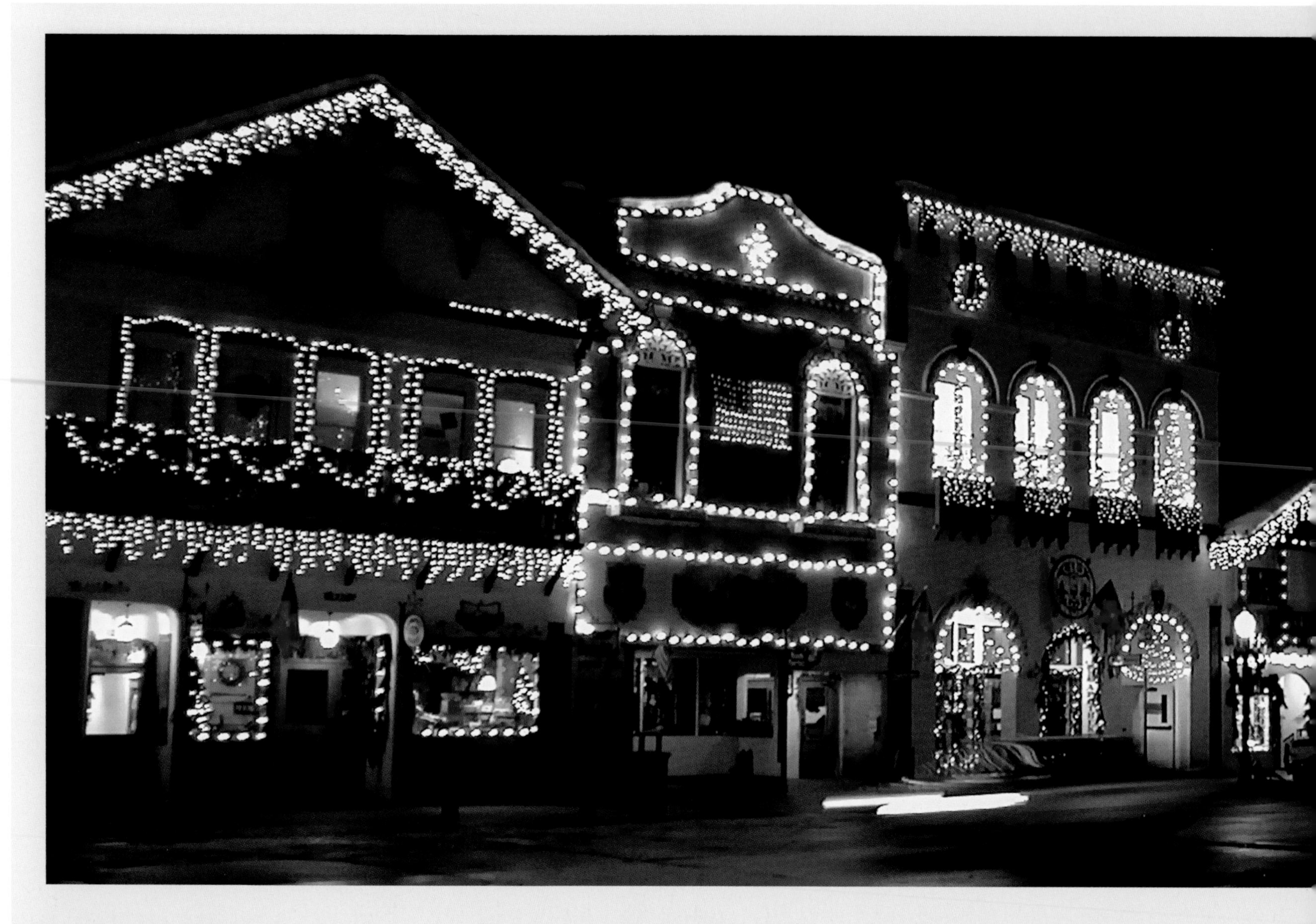

Bavaria in the Pacific Northwest

The world of amusement parks has plenty of "themed attractions" — water parks, for instance, or even entire resorts inspired by cartoon or television characters. But outside of historical recreations like Colonial Williamsburg, you rarely find an entire themed city.

Rarely, but not never. In central Washington, about a third of the way from Seattle to Spokane, stands a sliver of old Bavaria called Leavenworth. When the railroad and timber industries that had supported the town began to fall away in the 1960s, the city fathers, possibly inspired by the Alps-like Cascade Mountains surrounding the town, transformed the place into a quintessential old Tyrolean village. Its buildings, even the local McDonald's, look like chalets or beer halls. The roofs extend well past the buildings' outer walls, and murals and slats of dark brown timber decorate their white stucco faces. The entire town could be considered a tribute to cuckoo clocks, lederhosen, and bratwurst. And lights.

Front and Center

Front Street, Leavenworth's main drag *(left)*, includes an American flag on its Germanic architecture. Even Front Street's park and gazebo *(below)* do not escape the lighting frenzy.

In December, as many as 40,000 visitors come to watch Leavenworth glow. Strings of lights outline buildings, windows, walls, and doors, while icicle bulbs hang from rooftops, window sills, and balconies. The town makes a big deal out of the event, with a Village Lighting Festival that starts at noon and includes music, dance groups, and a lantern parade.

Of course, the glare of electrified tungsten filaments isn't exactly reminiscent of Renaissance-era Munich, but no one seems to mind. In fact, the Bavarian atmosphere seems strangely complemented by the dazzling and enormous display. In Leavenworth, as in other small towns across the country, holiday lights trump everything.

Going Public

It's not just householders and neighborhood organizers who try to outlight each other. All manner of parks (amusement and otherwise), municipal buildings, retail stores, inns and hotels, and other public venues are touched by the madness. Holiday illuminations (tasteful and otherwise) are the raison d'être for some festivals and events. And some public places don't even plug in their lights. They put them in bags.

Christmas with Elvis

Jennings Osborne covers Graceland *(below* and *at right)* with more than two million lights. Surely the King would approve of the glamorous result.

Lights by the Million

Once there was a rich man named Jennings Osborne who decorated his estate in Little Rock, Arkansas. By the 1990s, his display had grown to more than three million lights and included trumpeting angels, a twirling globe, a gigantic tree, crosses and crowns and candles, and more.

But Osborne's neighbors didn't like the cars and crowds that his electric phantasmagoria drew, and they sued him. In 1994, the Arkansas Supreme Court ordered Osborne to dim down the display and take other actions to thin out the staring mobs.

Osborne took the case to the United States Supreme Court. The Court refused to hear the case. Even worse, the free-spending Osborne — he was once quoted as saying, "Moderation is not in my vocabulary" — went bankrupt in 1995. His light display seemed like a goner.

But then Osborne heard from a guardian angel, or at least a guardian mouse. The Walt Disney Company offered to install his display as a Christmas attraction at Walt Disney World's Disney-MGM Studios theme park.

Osborne grabbed the offer. Today, his display — part of which he still oversees — numbers more than five million bulbs.

The bulbs don't just light up the studio back lot. They completely cover its surfaces and landscaping, caking and encrusting every inch with bursts of color. There's not just a Santa here and there. The display has every holiday symbol, greeting, and cliché imaginable.

More than a hundred angels take wing, including a batch flying around a glowing carousel. A huge champagne bottle pops its cork next to letters wishing you a happy new year. Enormous cones of light in almost every color, three and four stories high, suggest Christmas trees on an acid trip. Mickey Mouse shakes hands with Santa Claus, both of them large enough to slug Godzilla. And whenever you think you've seen it all, there's more: a huge train made of lights, an angel visible only through 3D glasses, and the silhouette of Mickey's familiar head worked subtly into the design of an elaborate light arrangement.

Preparations for the Osborne-Disney display begin during the summer, as technicians test each of the millions of bulbs for burnout, discoloration, and weak wiring. Hanging up the lights takes more than two months. But the visitors don't care much about that, especially if they're present as dusk settles in and the display suddenly blasts into light.

As if that's not enough, Jennings Osborne has lit up Elvis Presley's Graceland for Christmas, as well as other places here and there. When you've got lights by the million, there's always a few to go around.

Park Power

Theme parks do a lot with lights, but they can be costly to visit. In contrast, you can see public parks on the cheap, and their displays often rival even the best of those in the private domain.

Take the Eckerd Celebration of Lights in the Pittsburgh-area park Hartwood Acres. Designed by a rock-'n'-roller — Eckerd lighting director Michael Steinmetz spent years illuminating heavy-metal concerts — the place is a powerhouse. It features more than two million lights on displays reaching up to 40 feet in height, and it's laid out over a trail running more than three miles from one end to the other. In 2000, winds blowing in excess of 60 miles per hour destroyed a bunch of the Eckerd displays; a day later, though, the show was up and shining.

The Eckerd Celebration isn't the only public-park colossus. For example, Jones Beach of Long Island, New York, puts on the Holiday Light Spectacular, which has more than a million bulbs and a hundred displays, including some designed by local high-school students. The results can get pretty strange; one year a Jones Beach display included dancing fish in Santa hats. Near Washington, D.C., Bull Run Regional Park of Centreville, Virginia, puts on the Miracle of Lights, a two-mile lighted stretch offering more than 250 displays, many of which are animated. One of the festival's sillier features is "Planet Holiday," wherein bands of Earth-bound aliens celebrate Christmas.

But monsters like these aren't easy to manage. The St. Louis suburb of Alton, Illinois, puts on a Celebration of Christmas that includes over two million lights and has attracted more than half a million visitors. Nevertheless, the organizers have talked about killing the event due to its considerable costs.

Texas's Prairie Lights, in the Dallas suburb of Grand Prairie, wound a three-mile course through Lynn Creek Park that included about four million lights and more than 500 displays. Born during the middle 1990s, the event grew so popular that it spawned the spin-off Northern Lights in the town of Allen, north of Dallas. But Prairie Lights must have been too much to handle. In 2002, Grand Prairie's civic leaders sold it to High Point Church in Arlington, a few miles west of Grand Prairie.

The moral? In the long haul, a place with a smaller number of bulbs may have a better chance of survival, especially if its offerings stand out from the predictable lights-festival slate of reindeer and elves.

General's Stars

In Cleveland's Nela Park, the holiday lighting display sponsored by General Electric *(above)* shows off some of the products that made the company famous.

Bright Nights, Indeed

The Bright Nights show at Forest Park in Springfield, Massachusetts, may awe its human spectators, but the horses seem more interested in their own conversation.

Botanic Bizarre

If you think that plants are the only attractions municipal botanical gardens have on display, you are sadly mistaken. In fact, botanical gardens across the country offer some of the most beautiful holiday lights displays a lowly sightseer could want. One hopes the permanent denizens of the gardens — that is, the plants — enjoy the show as much as the rest of us.

New Mexico's biggest holiday lights show, for example, takes place at Albuquerque Biological Park, and features animated plants and animals, including a handsome but eerie cactus and skull *(above)*. The Garden D'Lights show at Washington's Bellevue Botanical Gardens, near Seattle, employs 400,000 bulbs in, naturally, the shapes of flowers and vines *(right)*. And at Tucson Botanical Gardens' Luminaria Nights *(far right)*, 2,000 bags with lit candles are put on display for three evenings of sightseeing and entertainment.

Shopping Madness

Passersby in this Tokyo shopping center stand transfixed by gargantuan reindeer and blinding wattage (a display that's doubly impressive considering that Japan is largely non-Christian).

Municipal Madness

When government leaders propose to decorate a park, they can justify the expense by saying that they're encouraging the citizenry to use and enjoy municipal recreational facilities, thereby doing a service for the community. But when they light up the building that contains their own offices, they're just showing off.

But without such showoffs, Denver wouldn't have the spectacle of its stunning City and County Building. The building, a multicolumned Greek temple rising three stories high and topped by a beaux-arts

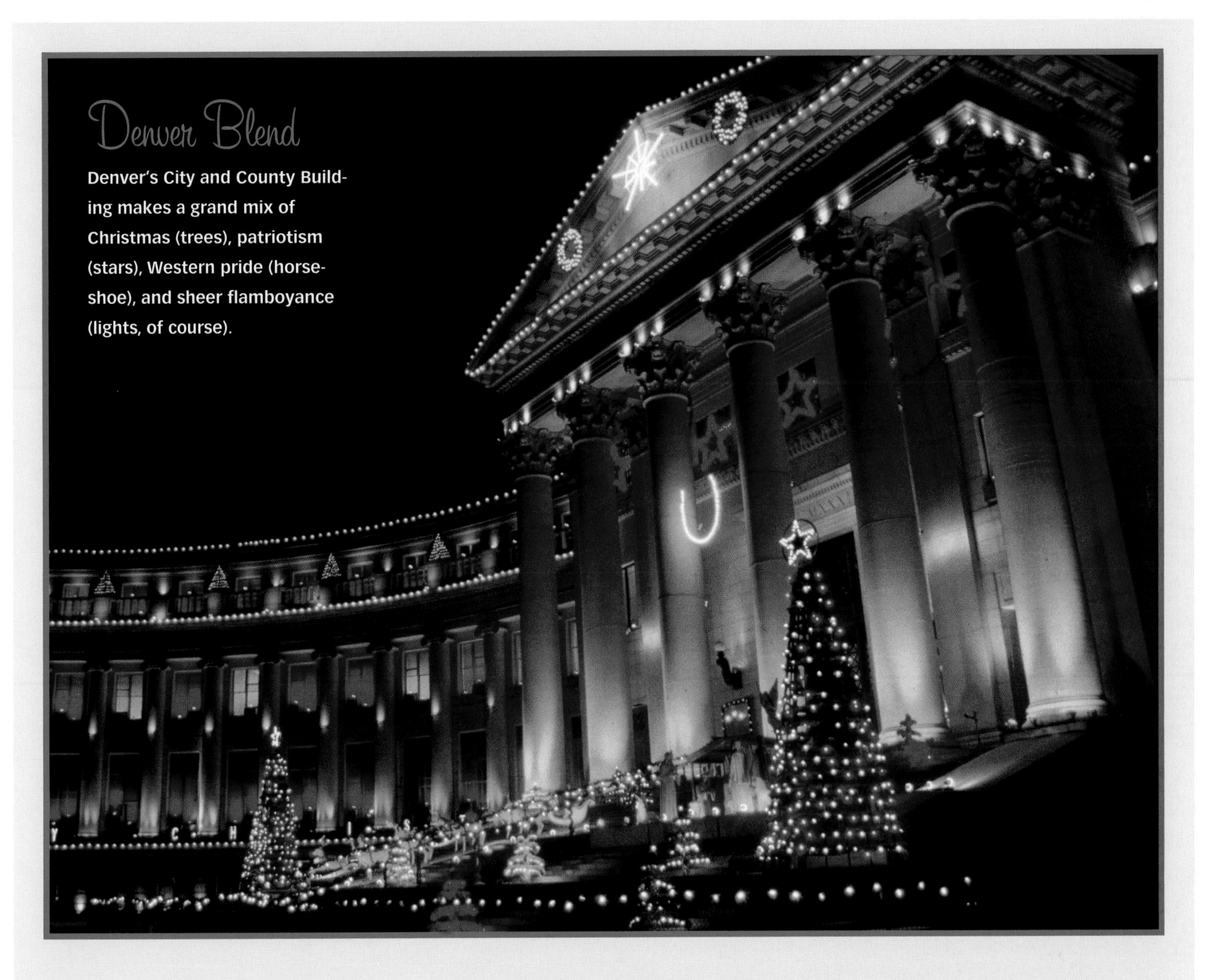

Denver Blend

Denver's City and County Building makes a grand mix of Christmas (trees), patriotism (stars), Western pride (horseshoe), and sheer flamboyance (lights, of course).

tower, forms a wide arc, its right and left wings curving forward to surround visitors with civic power. The building is lined with conventional Christmas lights; the lights also form wreaths and stars that hang between some of the building's columns and in other spots.

The real show, though, is floodlights, hundreds of them. They blast red, yellow, and green straight up the dozens of Corinthian columns that stand along the front of the building like giant warriors. The floods turn this dignified neoclassical edifice into a shameless psychedelic show that one might expect in Berkeley or Hollywood, not sensible Denver. It's the most wildly lit city hall in America, and possibly the world.

Not that others aren't holding their own. Honolulu's city hall wishes its citizens *Mele Kalikamaka* (Merry Christmas) with a two-ton sculpture of Shaka Santa giving the surfer's "hang loose" sign, a fist with pinky and thumb extended. He and Tutu Mele (Mrs. Claus), who wears a muumuu and lei, dip their feet into the City Hall fountain. Nearby stands a 50-foot Christmas tree that in some years is decorated with musical instruments, including (of course) ukeleles.

Other towns prefer a simpler approach, using nothing but plain white lights. But there's nothing at all plain about what they do with them, especially in Texas and Arkansas. In Little Rock, the Arkansas state capitol building covers its columns, dome, pediment, and parts of the walls in light while leaving other areas dark, creating striking patterns of brightness and blackness. It's part of a state-sponsored Trail of Lights that leads travelers from one municipal glow-fest to another.

In Marshall, Texas, the Harrison County Courthouse and its surrounding trees glow as though they invented luminescence. The display is an elaborate one, with strings of bulbs outlining the courthouse's architectural details. When *County*, the Texas' Association of Counties' magazine, did a cover story titled "Courthouses Don Holiday Lights," Marshall's courthouse was on the front page.

A few hundred miles southwest, in Johnson City, the Blanco County Courthouse features rivers of filigree along its roof's edge, with waves of bulbs that crest and droop like fancy stitching. Ropes of light hang from roof to ground, surrounding the place in a drape of lights. Even the chimneys get done up fancy, with horizontal stripes of bulbs that make them resemble Dr. Seuss's Cat in the Hat's stovepipe topper. To a defendant approaching the courthouse with fears of losing his finances or freedom, nothing says "This institution takes your case seriously" like a courthouse that looks like a whimsical wedding cake.

Clauses on Holiday

The Clauses — and a portly little friend — take in some rays at Honolulu's City Hall fountain.

Street Scenes

In some towns, the city fathers and mothers go for the simple but decorative approach: They light up the trees. Chicago's Magnificent Mile Lights Festival is one of the best-known lit-tree projects. A million lights are strung in the two hundred trees that line Michigan Avenue. The first lighting of these trees is always a key moment of the season.

But the most famous avenue of lit trees is probably Paris's Champs Elysees, the massive boulevard that leads to the Arc de Triomphe. People come from all over the world to see and photograph the lights that climb the up-reaching branches of these well-known elms. A picture of them in full brightness even heads up the street's official website.

Is Paris really the city of lights? The trees think so.

The Urban Forest

A nighttime view of the Champs Elysees *(below)* during the holiday season shows the trees garnished with enough lights to make them seem afire. Elsewhere in Paris, electric stars *(left)* loom large over city streets.

Bright Lights, Big Everything

Trees at New York's Rockefeller Center *(left)* help skaters see what they're plowing into. Toy soldiers protect the tree at Radio City *(inset).* Even the Empire State *(below)* gets in the spirit.

Going Commercial

Cities light up for prestige, tourism, civic pride, or any number of other reasons. But businesses, even though they too are sometimes driven by a need for prestige or other intangibles, usually put up lights for another reason: profit. The lights are a way to entice and attract customers.

Surprisingly, some of the brightest shows are found among the most dignified institutions of business and finance. This seems to be especially true in New York City. The immense columns in front of the New York Stock Exchange blaze brightly every December; in the patriotic year 2001, their lights formed an American flag. The Empire State Building turns a variety of colors every holiday season, while both Rockefeller Center and Radio City light up enormous trees and put up sculptures of angels, toy soldiers, wrapped gifts, and a variety of other holiday favorites.

The phenomenon isn't limited to Manhattan, of course. Bankers Hall in Calgary, Alberta, for instance, has hung strings of golden lights that seem to go on into infinity. For a structure with so conservative a name, it's a strangely ethereal show, but a welcome one.

Spend Money Here!

With its rows of white lights, Harrods in London *(above)* combines flash with dignity.

Bulbs Around the Block

Retail stores, of course, are especially famous for lights displays. For many of them, the holiday season is the big time of year, accounting for half or more of their annual sales. Nervously aware that fickle customers can take their money elsewhere, retailers get passionate about attracting customers by any means electrical. From Harrods in London, which takes up an entire city block and rims nearly every line of its exterior in lights, to Macy's in New York, which strings up an array of lights to create the silhouette of a Christmas tree on its face, stores love to go bright.

While individual stores may go bright, entire shopping districts go blinding. Unfortunately for fans of the extreme, retail displays get no funkier than Religions of the World, an ecumenically correct area with light sculptures of various faiths' symbols. It belongs to the International Festival of Lights in Battle Creek, Michigan, which to its credit pulls more than 200,000 spectators a year. More than a mere retail event, the festival of more than a million lights (most of them plain white) takes in all of Battle Creek's downtown, including the local zoo and the headquarters of the Kellogg cereal company.

A little bit looser is San Antonio's River Walk, where multihued bulbs bedeck bridges, trees, and businesses along the San Antonio River. River Walk is something of a party street even without lights — a popular national jazz radio show, "Live from the Landing," has originated there — and the extra dash of color from the lights simply spices the night.

A slightly more eccentric celebration is Milwaukee's Holiday Lights Festival. The 2002 event included a "Santa at Sea" section, with familiar holiday characters enjoying life on the oceans and even under them. There was also something that a local website called "amazing and rather funky for Milwaukee": the Techno-Tree Forest, wherein computer-controlled lights played patterns cued to music onto a gang of trees covered in fabric.

Branson, Missouri, being a town devoted to entertainment (it's the home of the Silver Dollar City theme park), should go wild with lights — and it does, in a way. Nearly every retail establishment, theater, and restaurant is lit up. But the best displays are the ones that have a touch of absurdity, like the row of snowmen and trees living quite cheerfully under a bridge. Or the Santa of lights riding a dinosaur that wears its own Santa hat. Or the unapologetically excessive 500 Christmas trees that stand along the two-mile Festival of Lights Parkway.

That's all good stuff. But for business districts that provoke a genuine sense of holiday wonder, you have to leave the United States.

City Splendor **San Antonio's River Walk *(bottom)* paints the town red (and yellow and green). Near Branson, Silver Dollar City theme park *(top)* lights up to enthrall visitors. And in Milwaukee's Zeidler Union Park, this giant red bear *(inset)* is a regular.**

Brits Get Lit

The overhead displays that straddle shopping streets in most American towns are pretty predictable: holly, wreaths, wrapped gifts, Santas, and such. Streets in England often feature designs that are just as conventional; stars seem to be a special favorite there. But thankfully, the English have sometimes lit their street decor with a touch of the bizarre.

In 1935, London's Paddington Station saw clowns flanking a Santa who fixed passersby with an incongruously cold, hard stare. By the early 1960s, fashionable Oxford Street was suspending oddly bulbous lanterns that looked like flying saucers, albeit flying saucers with flame-like tops and bottoms. In 1965, when Beatle-era England was at its most swinging, the hippest road in London was Carnaby Street, birthplace of the miniskirt. Overhead hung giant hearts emblazoned WITH LOVE FROM CARNABY STREET in curving, stretching letters.

In more recent times, unseasonal sunbursts have hung over Oxford Street, while Regent Street has erected floating chandeliers. In Alnwick, in the north of England near Scotland, setups include a mouse and cheese, the theatrical masks of tragedy and comedy, and the gear-shaped Rotary International symbol. In Newlyn, a seaside town on the English Channel in Cornwall, businesses have lit up a lobster, a mermaid, and letters shouting SAVE OUR FISH.

English eccentricity is alive and weird.

England Swings **During the holiday season, traffic in London's Regent Street shopping district is treated to dazzling displays.**

CHRISTKINDLMARKTS

A lot of modern Christmas is German. The piney Tannenbaum may have been born in the Black Forest, the name Claus (as in Santa) sounds pretty Teutonic, and "Silent Night" originated as the German "Stille Nacht." It seems only natural that the Germans have their own version of holiday lights.

The lights blaze especially brightly at the Christkindlmarkts. These open-air bazaars for selling Christmas gifts, ornaments, and foods fill public squares all over Germany. They're incredibly popular; Munich and Nuremberg, which have the oldest Christmas markets, draw literally millions of people.

Virtually any town of any size has a Christmas market. Cologne has more than one, the most prominent of which is held at the foot of the town's 750-year-old cathedral. More than a hundred pavilions and stalls brighten the night while collecting the customers' deutschmarks. About 70 miles north of Cologne, an enormous canopy of white lights, like a floating circus tent, hangs over the Christmas market in Essen. To the west of Essen, the Christmas market in Dortmund features what may be the world's biggest Christmas tree — well above 100 feet tall, made of more than 1,000 spruce trees and decorated with over 10,000 lights.

The tradition has stretched beyond Germany. Nearby cities such as Austria's Salzburg and France's Strasbourg have set up their own Christmas markets. So have faraway places like London's Covent Garden and the town with the blazing city hall, Denver.

But the Germans do it best.

Zoo Lights

Animals big and small, fearsome illuminated sculptures, hundreds of thousands of lights, and a backdrop of nighttime darkness. Mix them all together and what do you have? Zoo lights: a holiday lights display guaranteed to delight, entice, and otherwise enthrall visitors of all ages and persuasions.

Animal Alert

At the Denver Zoo, giant paw prints cast by flood-lights dwarf visitors *(above left)*, lights strung in trees *(bottom left)* seem to be fantasy crea-tures escaping captivity, and dragonflies are drawn to a spider's fatal web *(above)*. At the Phoenix Zoo, a shy rhino *(top right)* offers visitors only his portly rear end. And the entrance to the Port Defiance Zoo in Tacoma *(right)* is almost enough to scare off visitors.

Do Not Stare Directly at the Hotel

Of all the businesses that use lights as an attraction, few are as proud of it as hotels and resorts. Apparently, quite a few travelers enjoy sleeping near the sizzle of burning filaments.

It's hard to blame them. The Mission Inn, a century-old landmark in the southern California city of Riverside, does more than just put up a bunch of lamps. It throws a two-million-bulb Festival of Lights. The inn's immense grounds feature 200-plus lit figures, including man-size trumpeting angels, golden elves, and a Santa Claus trying to crawl into one of the hotel's chimneys. Guests at the inn also encounter animated trolls, an oddly Scandinavian touch for a place that looks like a Spanish cathedral. The season's first flipping of the switch to ignite the lights is itself a grand tourist attraction, drawing more than 10,000 people.

Further south, just off the coast of San Diego, lies the town of Coronado and the Hotel Del Coronado, which Hollywood has made famous. The hotel has appeared

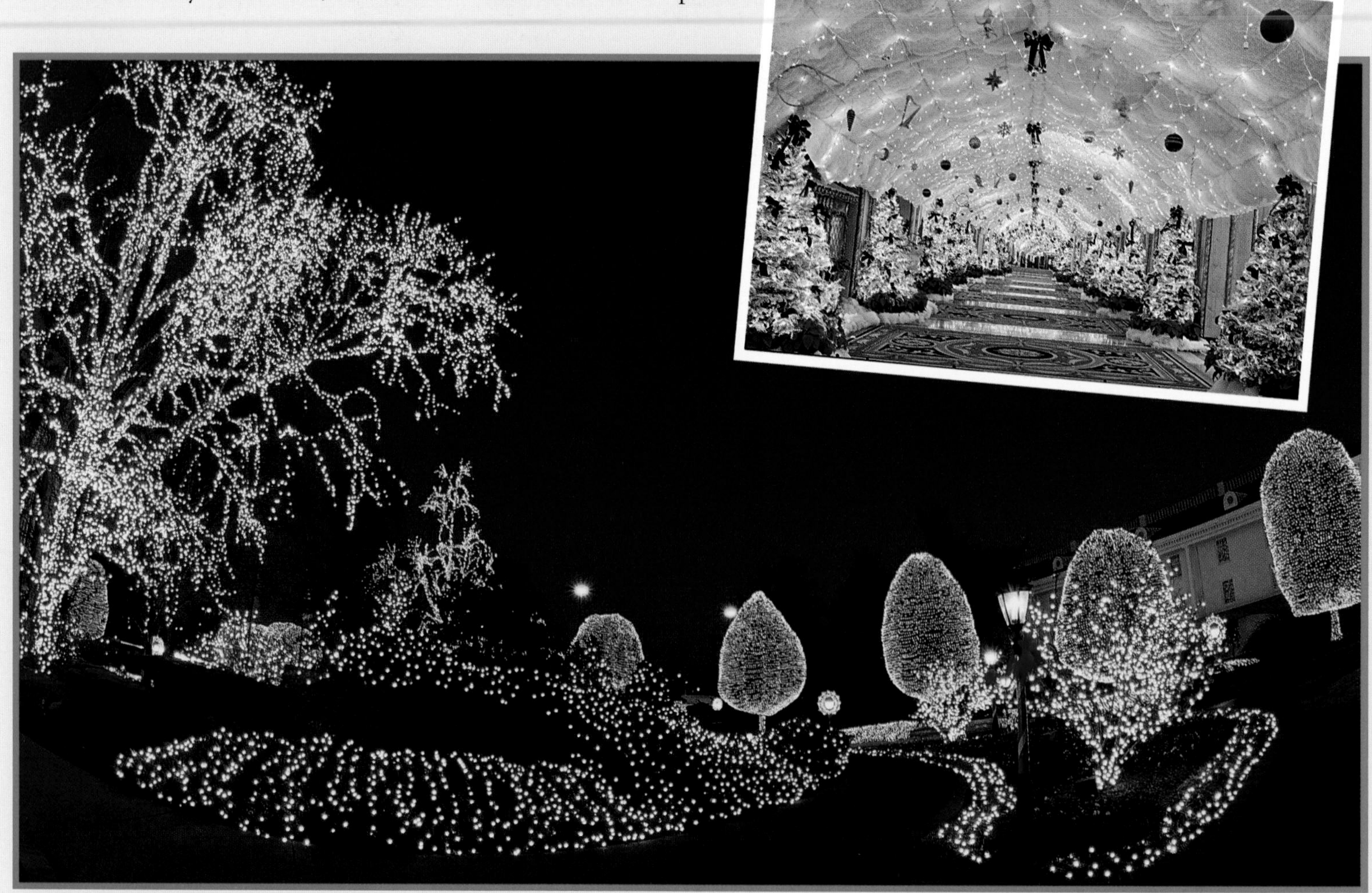

Ho-ho-hotels **Is it heaven or New Orleans? The Fairmont Hotel's block-long canopy *(inset)* could make one wonder. And the exterior of Nashville's Opryland Hotel *(above)* is almost enough to rival the Fairmont's interior.**

in a number of films, most notably the Marilyn Monroe comedy *Some Like It Hot*. While the Del, as some people call it, doesn't have as many lights as the Mission Inn, it uses its 50,000 bulbs well, streaming them along the roofs and facades. But if you want to stay there, be rich. Room rates start at well above $200 per night and rise to more than $2,000 for a beachside bungalow.

American hotels don't have a corner on lights. The gorgeous but quirky Kanucha Bay Resort, on Okinawa near the U.S. Marine installation Camp Schwab, is a luxury hotel that offers a golf course and indoor and outdoor swimming pools but also attracts environmentally conscious tourists who want to experience East Asia's unspoiled wilds. What's more, the hotel has erected on its grounds a full-scale duplicate of former President Bill Clinton's boyhood home in Hope, Arkansas. Given Kanucha Bay's reputation for indulging in such oddities, it should come as no surprise that in 2001, the hotel put up 700,000 lights on (among other things) more than 2,000 trees. The bulbs' reflection off the surface of the resort's bodies of water doubles their glow and makes the experience even more impressive.

Back in the United States, New Orleans's Fairmont Hotel has found a different way to hang lights. The hotel stretches a cottony white canopy over its lobby, and from that canopy it hangs tens of thousands of ornaments and lights. Lit-up Christmas trees line the walls and pour even more radiance into the scene. Walking the lobby is like strolling within an incandescent cloud, although one suspects that the hotel's visitors may be grateful when they get out of it. The lobby runs the length of a city block.

Christmas Lanterns

In jazzy New Orleans, even the trees have the blues. The Celebration in the Oaks festival in City Park manages to be both festive and spooky.

Lights in Bags

Down Mexico way, they've got a different way to light up. Combining paper and open flame, it sounds like a recipe for charred and smoky neighborhoods —but not when done right.

Farolito, the more traditional term for this object, means "small lantern." *Luminaria*, the more common name in the United States, comes from a word meaning "small bonfire." Either way, it's the same thing: a paper bag, inside of which are a lit candle and some sand to anchor the bag and candle in place. Hispanic immigrants brought the luminaria tradition to the United States, where it has become popular. The little bags produce a soft glow that many people adore.

People place luminarias along a walkway or rooftop — usually. Rows of luminarias have lined the quad at the University of Alabama, surrounded an old cannon and historical marker during the Nights of Lights festival in St. Augustine, Florida, and followed a riverfront in Galena, Illinois. In New Mexico, they've decorated Santa Fe's prominent and ancient-looking Inn of Loretto and illuminated gravesites in Albuquerque.

New Mexico, in fact, is ground zero for American luminarias. In that state, more people place and light more luminarias than you'd ever want to count. For really big numbers, though, few places can beat the 5,000 that Boy Scout Troop 427 of Solomons Island, Maryland, have put out as a service to the community, or the 7,000 that attract visitors to the Desert Botanical Gardens in Phoenix.

The American love for innovation being what it is — and what it is can be pretty wacky — the traditional mix of bag, sand, and candle has undergone a few twists. Electric luminarias, with light bulbs in plastic bags, are readily available. The cable network Home and Garden Television has recommended luminarias made of chicken wire with strands of tiny holiday lights inside. Legally blind septuagenarian Ray Lee of Anchorage, Alaska, has used local materials to make "ice lanterns," stumpy cylinders of frozen water that take the place of paper bags. Like makers of traditional luminarias, Lee puts candles rather than electric bulbs inside his lanterns.

Since candles run down and die, traditional luminarias don't last long. Whether they're made of ice or paper, they can, frankly, be a chore and a bore to fill with sand and candle, put in place, and light up, one after another after another, night after night. Consequently, some places set out their bags only on Christmas Eve or the Saturday night before the eve.

So don't be surprised if you're walking the dog one late December night and you find a formerly dark pathway that's suddenly become a river of small fires. Just keep the dog's nose out of the bags.

Desert Blooms **The Mormon Temple in Mesa, Arizona, rivals the setting sun.**

Blazing with Holiness

Amid all of this mad decorating, whatever happened to the origins of the season? Lights on hotels and department stores are all very pretty, but the holidays that they celebrate started with religious observance. Where are the churches in all of this glare?

Some of them are providing their own glare. The Mormon Temple in Mesa, Arizona, has been lighting up since 1980, a job that involves hundreds of volunteers. Its 600,000 lights attract more than a million visitors every year. Since Mesa, like Bethlehem, is located in a desert, the temple's meticulously sculpted, realistically colored, subtly lit, full-size outdoor Nativity scene can give spectators the spooky sense that "this is what it was really like."

In Belleville, Illinois, near St. Louis, stands the National Shrine to Our Lady of the Snows, owned and operated by the Missionary Oblates of Mary Immaculate. (An oblate is someone who lives in a religious community.) During the holiday season, close to one million miniature bulbs cover the shrine's foliage and illuminate life-size figures and displays — or as the shrine's website describes them, "electro-art sculptures" — in scenes from the life of Jesus. People who don't want to drive through the mile and a half of lights can view them from the shrine's trolley or a horse-drawn carriage, or they can simply escape the lights by taking in a show at the shrine's theater. And you thought a shrine would be somber and restrained.

Somber and *restrained* are not words usually applied to Trinity Broadcasting Network. TBN broadcasts 24-hour televangelism worldwide from its own Vatican-style complex, Trinity Christian City International, in the affluent and conservative southern California community of Costa Mesa. Every winter, TBN also broadcasts the wattage of 750,000 lights into the skies. Even when California hit an energy crisis in 2000, the TBN lights stayed ablaze. However, with encouragement from Costa Mesa's mayor and picketing protestors, TBN did make the concession of reducing the lights' schedule from all night to the hours between 8 P.M. and midnight.

In Albuquerque, New Mexico, the San Felipe de Neri church hasn't skipped a Sunday service in nearly three hundred years, but most people forget about that grand history when they catch sight of the church's lights. Every Christmas Eve, San Felipe de Neri puts out hundreds of luminarias. Forming a cross in the church's yard, running along its pathways, and lining the building's rooftops and arches, the luminarias wash the church in a warm yellow glow.

Now that's spiritual.

Menorahs for the Masses

People who set up public holiday celebrations aren't always sure what to do with Jewish holidays. Most Jewish holidays aren't big on hoopla; even the most important one, Yom Kippur, is a time of fasting and solemn repentance. And though Hanukkah is the festival of lights, the lights come in small numbers, just enough to fill a menorah. Except for a supersized public menorah here or there, most Jews don't go in for big holiday light displays.

But there are exceptions. As noted in the introduction, Texas's Moody Gardens Festival of Lights includes a menorah and Jewish stars. At Forest Park in Springfield, Massachusetts, the Bright Nights show features a similar display: an 18-foot menorah and several Stars of David, all made out of lights. (Bright Nights, by the way, is very ecumenical. It's one of the few places to have a display honoring Kwanzaa.) And of course some displays avoid the entire issue of religion by sticking with cartoon characters and snowmen.

Individual homeowners, though, do like to honor Judaism. In Austin, 37th Street lights founder Jamie Lipman has put up a menorah and Stars of David by his front door. Near Atlanta, householders Lee and Karen Lockridge reportedly put a Star of David, an Islamic crescent moon, and a Christian cross in their display to encourage peace on earth after the September 11 terrorist attacks. And in the heavily Jewish city of Miami, a big, 4,000-light display has deployed dreidels, Jewish stars, and other symbols. A special feature of the display was a row of lights-topped sticks or bars in the shape of a menorah.

Displays like these aren't exactly the volcanic eruptions of electric fireworks that grace some other places — but that may be all for the best. Jews are supposed to say a prayer when lighting menorahs or other holiday lights. Even the most devout Jew might not want to contemplate the prayers for a display of lights numbering in tens of thousands.

Lights on the March

Not every lights display stays in one place. A lot of them walk and roll. Mickey Mouse usually serves as the master of ceremonies for the late-November parade of Chicago's Magnificent Mile Lights Festival. The floats are big and sometimes goony — McDonald's, for instance, has sent a giant Ronald McDonald shoe motoring down the street. But there's more to the show than the floats. Stage shows, ice carving demonstrations (with buzzsaws on huge hills of ice), and other sights precede the parade, and fireworks follow it. The event pulls thousands of Midwesterners to Chicago's downtown — quite a feat considering how cold Chicago can get in November.

Minneapolis is even colder, so its Holidazzle parade allows spectators to reserve heated chairs called Hot Seats. Running every weekend from Thanksgiving to late December, the Holidazzle features floats in mock fairy-tale themes, bearing titles such as "Santabear and Mrs. Santabear" and "Nutcracker Doodlebug." A specialty of the show is the large dancing bulbs: people stuffed inside huge colored lights and hoofing their way down the street. The entire affair is simultaneously cute, kitschy, admirable, and utterly surreal.

There are other big-city holiday parades of note, but for floats that reflect a citizenry's true character, one has to hit smaller communities — and especially, for some reason, Canadian ones. In Rockwood, Ontario, the Farmers' Santa Claus Parade of Lights is composed of lights-covered tractors and other farm vehicles, plus a dancing stable cleaner and, in the grand finale, Santa and Mrs. Claus riding a combine. The Santa Claus Parade of Chilliwack, British Columbia, has included among its marchers the Fraser Valley Llama and Alpaca Club; the club's four-hooved members wore the lights. And the Parade of Lights in Nipawin, Saskatchewan, has featured a hockey player made of lights; a hammer as big as a truck, outlined in lights (sponsored by a local lumber company); and a float displaying plastic gallon jugs with lights inside and a sign saying RECYCLE MILK CONTAINERS. You don't get that sort of down-home stuff in colossal events like Macy's Thanksgiving Day parade. Too bad for Macy's.

Magnificence **Rivers of traffic on Chicago's Magnificent Mile form a nightly parade that halts only for the annual Lights Festival.**

Holidazzle

This Minneapolis parade includes floats, fairy-tale characters, and marching bands whose members do not escape the lighting frenzy.

Lights That Float

Keep electricity away from water, your mother told you. Well, she was probably wrong about other things, too.

Holiday boat parades are a grand triumph of indulgence over common sense. Owning and maintaining a private yacht is expensive enough, but creating an elaborate lighting display for a single night's cruise edges into sheer extravagance.

The tradition seems to have started in 1907, when Italian gondolier John Scarpa started taking visitors for evening trips across southern California's Newport Harbor in a gondola lit by Japanese lanterns. The next year, Scarpa and other boatmen put on a small parade of illuminated boats. The practice caught on.

These days, the Christmas Boat Parade in Newport Harbor involves up to 150 boats. Since the harborside town of Newport Beach is one of America's wealthiest communities, the boats and their lights get pretty fancy. A light-draped volcano that shoots geysers of flame; a huge, moving bumblebee; a disco-like ship firing green lasers into the sky; a "flag ship" with Old Glory trim and Christmas trees lit in red, white and blue; and a yacht with palm trees, a sun, and the lettering SANTA'S CABO VACATION — these are typical sights for a Newport December.

In Florida, more than 800,000 people converge every year for Fort Lauderdale's Winterfest Boat Parade, and with good reason. The event is not so much a nautical convoy as an excuse for a party (as if anyone in Fort Lauderdale needed an excuse). Everyone from the Rotary Club to the Gay Business Alliance to the South Florida Divers SCUBA Club gets involved; all told, they sponsor about a hundred illuminated entries. The event is so vivid — Winterfest even encourages the homes and businesses along the parade route to

Newport Red

When Newport Harbor adorns itself in lights, it takes on a red hue — whether from embarrassment or party glow, one does not hazard to ask.

Lights Ahoy!

Sails of lights won't pick up much wind, but any boat parade would be happy to include these sporty little numbers.

light up — that it's one of the few holiday boat parades televised to communities all over America.

A preppier parade launches from the Eastport Yacht Club of Annapolis, Maryland. With boats named *Panache, Black Tie Affair,* and *Tres Jolie,* it's an event for the gentry, and they go at it with flair. In 2002, for instance, the powerboat *Oyster Stew* featured a cartoon Snoopy being towed in a dinghy, which sank after it passed the parade judges' reviewing stand. *Island Girl* showed off the illuminated image of a hula dancer, along with a real dancer whose clothes were made of lights. *Dauntless* displayed the Three Wise Men following the Star of Bethlehem. But the Wise Men may not all have been so wise; one of them was SpongeBob Squarepants.

They Put Lights on That?

Holiday lighters will cover anything in bulbs: gingerbread houses (never mind that the frosting might melt), construction cranes, even two 12-foot satellite dishes atop the University of Wisconsin at Madison's Atmospheric, Oceanic, and Space Sciences building. In Royal Oak, Michigan, a suburbanite tied lights around a mannequin and dangled it from her home, leading neighbors to call the cops about what they thought was a man in a horrible house-decorating predicament.

And that's just for starters.

Traditionally, holiday lights are a phenomenon seen on homes, whether they're white candles in the windows of staid colonials or wild tangles of lights and figures reminiscent of a circus tent. But not all homes are houses. Plenty are trailers and mobile homes, or even yurts and camps. And their owners put out plenty of lights.

Take, for example, a mobile home in Brandon, Florida, that has been a festival of illuminated Christmas images, including a Nativity scene, Santa and Mrs. Claus, a snowman, reindeer, angels, elves, and toy soldiers. Call the display a batch of clichés, but it's as complete a batch as you're likely to find. In Santa Rosa, California, a trailer in the Valle Vista III mobile home park has featured an animated display including dolls skating on a pond, teeter-tottering chipmunks, and mice grabbing a snowman's gloves. In Escondido, California, Betty Anderson not only blankets her trailer's exterior in lights but also displays a collection of 800 dolls. Her home has become a tourist attraction.

Even alien life forms can join in. On September 17, 1979, "a bizarre-looking object [hung] motionless in the southern sky" over the Gulf of Mexico, according to the website of the National UFO Reporting Center. "It had a row of lights horizontally across the center, of every color . . . The rectangular object looked like a flying mobile home made of silver with a string of Christmas lights wrapped around it." After a few moments, the object reportedly flew away.

Galactic sightseers? Or lights enthusiasts, come just a wee bit early for the holiday season?

The Lonely Night **Forlorn strands of lights adorn an old-fashioned trailer on the prairie *(top)*. In the stark fields of Alaska, a campsite *(left)* celebrates the season. Even an igloo *(right)* can be festive.**

Animal House

Should humans keep lights to themselves? Some people say no.

In Seattle's Magnolia neighborhood, lighters have lit a chicken coop with 14,000 bulbs. To the south, in Puyallup, Washington, a farmer has decorated his barn with gigantic lit-up lollypops, candy canes, and gingerbread men. Barns are so popular as lights sites that Breyer Horses — a company selling gifts for horse lovers — features a barn-decorating kit with stockings, wrapped packages, and, of course, lights.

But back to Puyallup, where near the barn is a lighted doghouse. It's not the only one. In Mendota, California, former general contractor Ed Petry built a duplex doghouse and used holiday lights to heat its top story. Faithful Friends (a volunteer organization in League City, Texas, that brings pets to visit people in nursing homes) put lights on a wheeled doghouse, tied it to a Siberian Husky, and put dog and house in the town's 2000 Christmas Parade.

Do the animals like the lights? Maybe not. But the people who light up their homes certainly do.

Birdhouse Beautiful

Putting the effort into decorating a birdhouse so elaborately seems a little compulsive — but also kind of cute.

Fingers of Light

In the Sonoran Desert near Tucson, Arizona, saguaro cacti point straight up as if trying to share their lights with the starless sky.

Plants with Bulbs

Next to the traditional Christmas tree, the cactus is the plant most likely to get lit up. Lights may actually preserve cacti, according to the website of the nursery Arizona Cactus Sales: "Christmas lights (large bulb) . . . will help to keep plants warm, especially those large specimens that may be difficult to cover."

Lots of areas illuminate cacti. In Las Vegas, for instance, confectioner Ethel M Chocolates lights up its popular Botanical Cactus Gardens in November and December. In Reno, Nevada, the Blue Cactus Bar & Nightclub has covered the cactus-shaped wooden cutouts lining its driveway with strand upon strand of lights. However, home base for electric cacti is surely Arizona. In Scottsdale, the Four Seasons Resort lights a nearby saguaro forest. In Chandler, a lit saguaro with five vertical branches looks like a luminous hand. So powerful is the pull of Arizona's electric cacti that when Arizonan Craig Borgen moved to Minnesota, he began building holiday displays that included cacti made from rebar.

The electric cacti's image appears on Christmas-tree ornaments from Hallmark, stamped in rhinestones on shirts from the "wearable art" company Sue's Sparklers, on greeting cards from Elite Concepts, and on patterns from the Needle Nook of La Jolla, a stitchery store near San Diego.

What is the appeal of electric cacti? The website of Anglicans Online may have an answer. "We laughed aloud the first time we saw a cactus with Christmas lights on it," said the December 2002 newsletter, "[but] the *locus classicus* for Advent symbolism is the 'Middle East,' with all its desert dryness and brilliant, blazing sun. If anything, it's northern hemisphere symbols that have gone awry . . . Perhaps a good exercise for each of us would be to look round throughout our worldwide communion and, from time to time, purposefully incorporate symbolism not of our own into our meditations."

And the electric cacti say, "Amen."

Movers and Shakers

Some bearers of lights want to be on the move.

Take, for example, *Let There Be LIGHTS!*, a Hyundai Elantra owned by Victor Engel of Austin, which he wired with over 400 bulbs. Lights near the rear window glowed when Engel braked; lights on the wheels flashed in time with his turn signals; lights on the bumper and hood brightened with the parking lights; and so on.

If you're no Engel, take heart. Vision Graphics, a North Carolina design firm, has drawn lights on vinyl strips that you can press onto your car. When headlamps shine on them at night, the lights' reflective paint shines back.

Like cars, bicycles are popular for lighting. Since lights need electricity that most bikes don't generate, many bulbed bikes exist only for display, not movement.

For movement, take trains. Canadian Pacific Railway, for instance, annually covers a locomotive in lights and sends it cross-country to gather donations for the Canadian Association of Food Banks. In 2002, it collected over $400,000 (Canadian) and 93 tons of food.

Then there are boats. It's not just lighted boat parades (see page 118) that grab the eye; it's the individual ships. A Vancouver tugboat has sported a reindeer head, with antlers, nearly as tall as the ship's mast. Off the coast of Massachusetts's Cape Cod, holiday lights have appeared on everything from a 12-foot skiff to the National Oceanic and Atmospheric Administration's big research vessel *Albatross IV*. And in December 2000, the Navy frigate U.S.S. *Thach*, stationed in San Diego, lit up in red, white, and green.

Anchors aweigh!

02
11
1

OUT-OF-SERVICE
GMC
OPEN
& BURGERS
TIFFANY'S
RESTAURANT
&
LUBE ROOM LOUNGE
WILLIAMS, ARIZONA
ARIZONA
US
66

Farmers' Follies

Even people who are hundreds of acres away from most witnesses like to show off. This tractor and truck are typical of displays by light fanatics living in agricultural country.

People Power

If setting out lights is a way to express yourself, then the ultimate place to put them is your own body.

For centuries, bullfighters have decked themselves out in the *traje de luces* — Spanish for "suit of lights," although it uses jewels rather than electric bulbs. During the vaudeville era, it's said, some performers wrapped themselves in lights, only to find their act go up in flames — literally. In the 1979 movie *The Electric Horseman,* Robert Redford played a rodeo champion forced into making a humiliating appearance on a Las Vegas stage; eventually, he rode out of Caesar's Palace and into the Nevada desert while wearing the high-powered jacket that gave the movie its name. In 1988, electronics engineer Rob Levitsky lit up a furry hide that he wore at Grateful Dead concerts. He took the suit to a December 1993 Christmas fashion show at the San Francisco nightclub Endup, where he was only one of many guests clad in light.

More recently, the small town of Pelzer, South Carolina, has spawned the Light People. For years, Pelzerites have sewn hundreds of lights onto their clothing, plugged the lights into extension cords, and powered up to wave at goggle-eyed passersby.

Meanwhile, Dangerous Interactive Systems of Berkeley, California — "an electronic design studio specializing in wearable interactive sculptures," says its website — has been developing its own suit of lights. It's a fireman's jacket covered in cool-glowing LED (light-emitting diode) bulbs that flash on and off in animated patterns. It's not ready for sale at this writing, but Dangerous Interactive hopes to make it available soon.

And who knows what other ways will come up to put lights on your body? In a world where women (and men, for that matter), paint themselves with makeup full of glitter, and children at amusement parks get temporary tattoos, it's not too hard to believe that some wild scientist will electrify the glitter or wire the ink to make them radiate like a Jennings Osborne fantasy — and keep the wearer warm amid the December snow. Maybe one future night, you'll stroll through your neighborhood, waving at a friend slathered in blinking red and green luminous body paint as a million tiny fiber optic dots turn your nose into a pointillist Christmas tree, an animated nativity scene plays across your forehead, and "Merry Christmas" flashes up one arm while "Happy New Year" chases down the other.

Ah, yes — better weirdness through technology.

Holidays

Building Your Own Display

So you want to create your own electrical extravaganza? Welcome to the jungle.

Frankly, there's a lot to learn about lights, and this book can't deliver it all. It'll get you started, though. And the appendix lists many resources you can turn to for help.

If you begin to doubt yourself, remember this: Thousands of people with less skill and experience than you have generated enough gaudiness that neighbors doubted their sanity, gawkers clogged their sidewalks, and the local news media treated them like carnival freaks. And with a little time, patience, and effort, all that can be yours!

Getting Started

For those who make building humongous holiday lights displays a lifelong hobby, networking with other lighting enthusiasts becomes a passion. But it's especially important when you're first getting started. Talk to people who have created their own displays. Find out what they would recommend you to do and especially what they recommend you avoid. They've learned from their mistakes; you should, too.

Start with your neighbors, if they light up. They know the advantages and perils of lighting up in your part of town. Besides, you may want to coordinate your lights display with theirs, creating a neighborhood-wide attraction.

Lighting enthusiasts tend also to be Internet enthusiasts, and the chat rooms of their websites (listed in the appendix; see page 178) are filled with friendly, helpful people. You should check them out. Often, the people who create displays are proud to reveal how they did it and give instructions.

Timing

Some who put up big lights displays start working in August or September. However, these early movers aren't motivated only by the time the job takes. Many confess that they love the whole process so much they can't wait to get started.

In any event, leave yourself enough days so that you don't stress yourself sweaty getting everything done at the last instant. Decide when you want to set the display ablaze; some lights enthusiasts flick the switch right after Thanksgiving, and others wait until days into December. Work backward from there. Designing, buying, and installing lights can take weeks or months, especially if you're new at the job and may need to redo things a few times to get them the way you want.

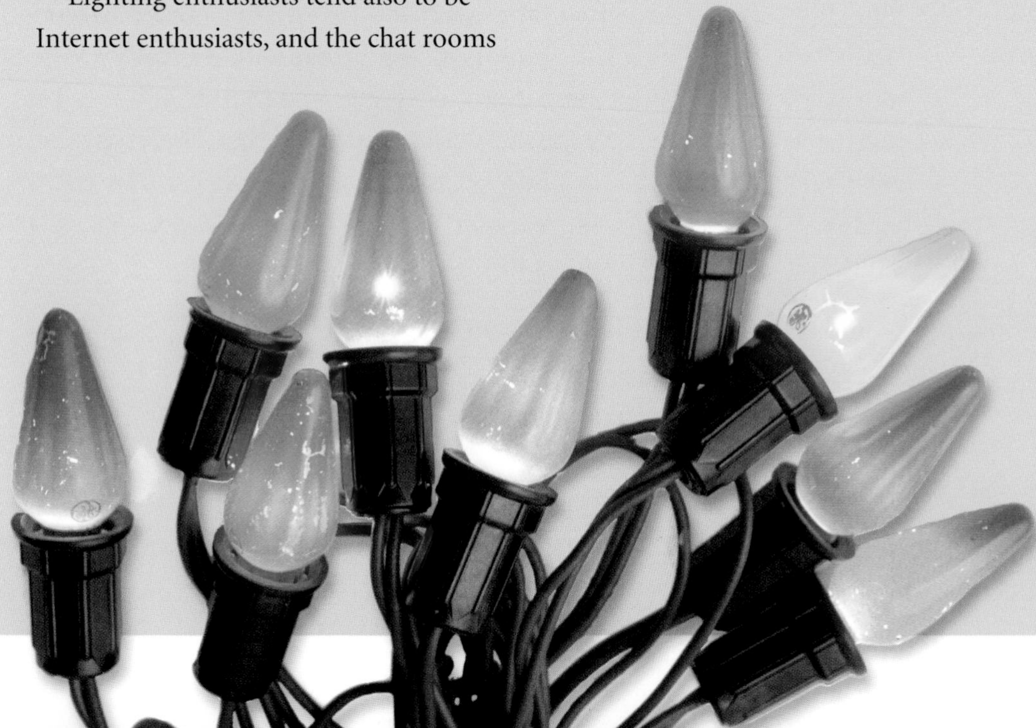

First-Timers

Start small. One lights enthusiast after another has said that he started with only a few lights. Even Jennings Osborne began with a fairly modest display, all in just one color (red).

As you begin to design your first display, focus on one particular item that you most want to highlight. "For example, if having lights on the roof is the most important item to consider, then design the roof lighting first, then build the remaining items around [it]," says Larry Brown, head of Christmas Pro Shop, a large holiday decorating firm.

Brainstorming

As you design your display, let your mind roam. Don't say no to any ideas, no matter how outlandish. Outlandish ideas can make for great displays, or at least lead you to concepts that are less wild but just as much fun.

Look for inspiration everywhere. Minneapolis's Paul Damon prays for his ideas. John Sesso of Old Bridge, New Jersey, gets the inspirations for his displays (more than 50,000 bulbs and counting) from the images in children's coloring books. "These are items a child can relate to," he says.

Growing

If all goes well, over time you may find yourself fantasizing of having a really big display. If you want one that can be seen at a distance — a block away, across the neighborhood, from Mars — consider this bit of advice from reporter Gaile Robinson of Knight-Ridder newspapers: "Outdoor lighting effects need to be big — really big. It may sound trite, but it's appropriate; they need to be as big as all outdoors. Life-size anything is too small."

If you decide to go really big, tell your neighbors. Show them your designs, especially if you plan to place lights on the property line between your home and theirs. This bit of initiative is common courtesy, it may prevent lawsuits, and it may even spur your neighbors into putting up their own displays.

DESIGNING YOUR DISPLAY

If you're working with a photo print, lay artist's tissue paper over it.

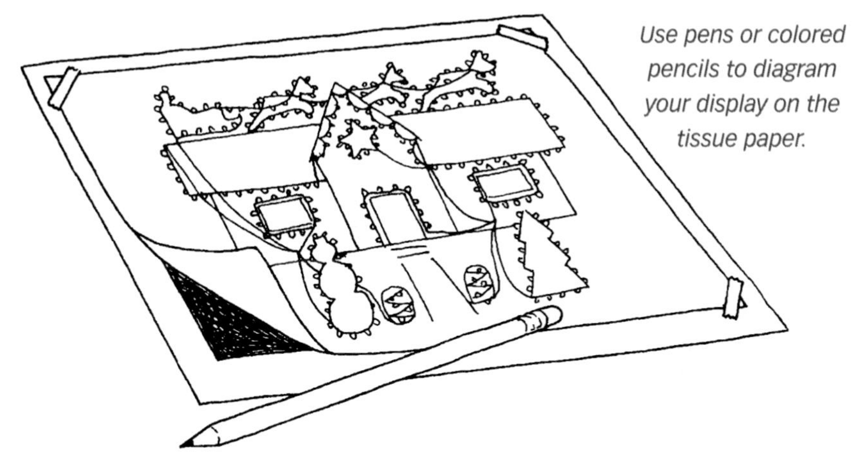

Use pens or colored pencils to diagram your display on the tissue paper.

Putting up a display is a lot easier if, before you go running around the yard tossing up lights and figurines left and right, you take the time to design your display on paper.

- **Take a picture of your home, and preferably several pictures from several angles. After all, your home should look good to anyone who sees it, no matter where they stand.**
- **Get your pictures developed or downloaded. If you have a digital camera, all the better, because manipulating pictures electronically can simplify your design process. If you use conventional film, you can get the pictures on screen by having Snapfish.com or another photo service develop them as electronic files, or you can get traditional prints and scan them. If you must work with prints, get several copies of each shot, and get them printed as big as possible.**
- **Now it's playtime. If the pictures are loaded on your computer, use one of the many photograph-manipulating software programs to draw lighting displays on your home. If you don't have such software, print out the pictures and draw on the pages. If you're working with photo prints, you can draw directly on them, but a less costly method is to draw on color copies of them (made at your local copy shop). You can also simply tape artist's tissue paper over the photo and sketch on that.**

Finding the Power

Once you've identified the places that you want to light, go look at them. Find the outdoor electrical outlets closest to those places, and mark them on your design. Generally speaking, it's best to put lights close to an outlet. If you don't have outlets near all the spots that you want to light, you'll need extension cords; better yet, have an electrician install more outlets.

To create a long row of lights, you may want to string a few strands of lights together. A household outlet can pump out only so many volts, however. Overloading it by forcing it to power up too many lights is dangerous.

But how many lights are too many? Most experts say three strands is the maximum. But if you need precise numbers, the state of California's energy commission has some advice: "Circuits in older homes carry a maximum of 1800 watts each. Most newer homes can handle 2400 watts each . . . To determine how many watts you're using, multiply the number of holiday bulbs by the number of watts per bulb. If you're not sure of the wattage, use 10 watts per bulb just to be safe!"

For really big lights displays, it's a good idea to work with an electrician. The electrician should check each of the outlets to make sure they're working properly and can supply all of the power that your design requires. If the existing outlets aren't enough, he should install extra outlets. Otherwise, you might plug too many lights into one outlet, overload the circuit, and cause a power failure or a fire. Another reason to get an electrician: Outdoor light arrays are likely to get wet, and an electrician can make sure that they won't electrocute anyone.

Each outlet should incorporate a ground fault circuit interrupter, or GFCI, which the United States Consumer Product Safety Commission calls "the most effective means for protecting consumers against electrical shock hazards." The presence of a GFCI is often marked by a little red rectangle between the upper and lower sets of holes on an electrical outlet. The safety commission's website explains, "A GFCI constantly monitors current flowing in a circuit to sense any loss of current. If the current flowing through two circuit conductors differs by a very small amount, the GFCI instantly interrupts the current flow to prevent a lethal amount of electricity from reaching the consumer. The consumer may feel a painful shock but will not be electrocuted." GFCIs are especially important for Christmas light displays, which face unpredictable weather and other hazards that can damage wires and lights.

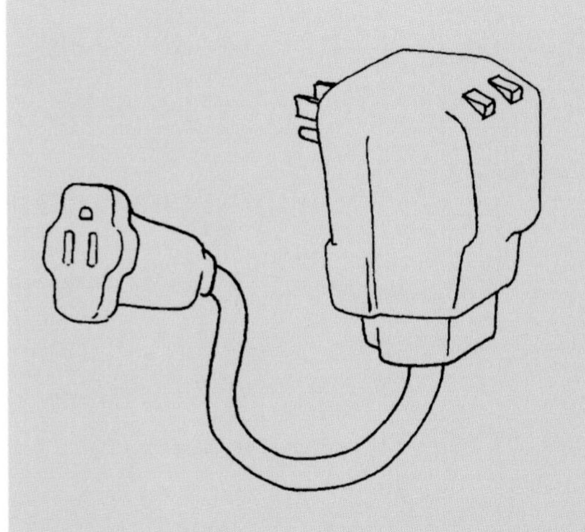

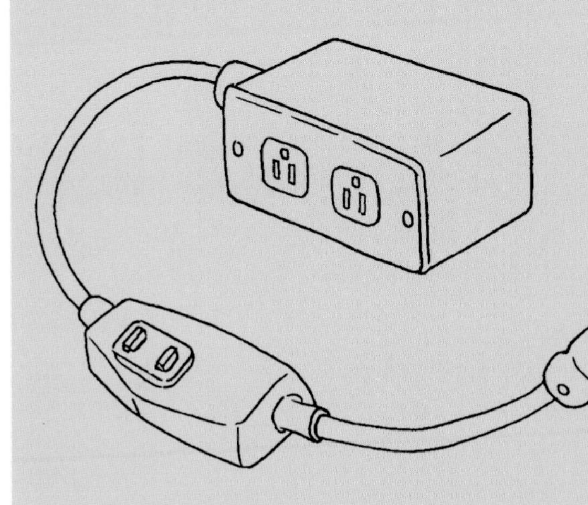

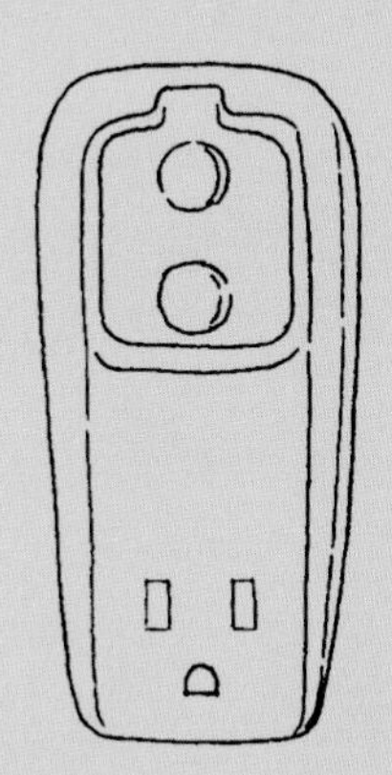

Plug-in GFCI outlets come in all shapes, sizes, colors, and configurations, including the three models shown above.

There are many different types of GFCIs. Some you can plug into an outlet yourself; others require an electrician. To be safe — always a good thing when dealing with electricity — ask your electrician to supply and install the device.

In order to make your lights glow, obviously you'll have to connect them to your outlets. You have now entered the world of extension cords and other items that control the flow of electricity.

Extension cords should be certified by Underwriters Laboratories and rated for outdoor use. Underwriters Laboratories (UL) is an independent, nonprofit company founded in 1894 to test electrical products for safety. The packaging of each extension cord you buy should display the UL seal. If you buy the wrong cord or one without the UL seal, it could overheat, starting a fire and turning your lovely yard into Front-Lawn Flambé.

Controlling the flow of electricity may be the most important job in a lighting display, but nearly as important is a very simple task: turning off the lights. You shouldn't let a display burn all night. If it does, it can overheat and ignite your home. But it's surprisingly easy to let your vigilance drop and neglect to shut down the power, especially after your display's been running trouble-free for a few nights. To prevent that mistake, consider installing a timer that will turn off your lights at whatever time you tell it to. The timer will come with its own instructions and in most cases will be fairly simple to operate.

Measure every place where you plan to lay lights, in the shapes and directions your lights will run. Will the lights line your eaves in a straight row or hang in curving swags? Will the lights travel over a flat surface or go over bay windows and other items that project outward? If you cover a tree in lights, do you want the "weeping willow" look that comes from hanging strings of light from its branches or the more organized sight achieved by wrapping the lights around the branches?

Doublecheck everything, and then check it again. Apply the handyman's credo "Measure twice, cut once": Measure your layout at least twice, so that you have to buy and install lights and extension cords only once.

Bulbs A-Plenty

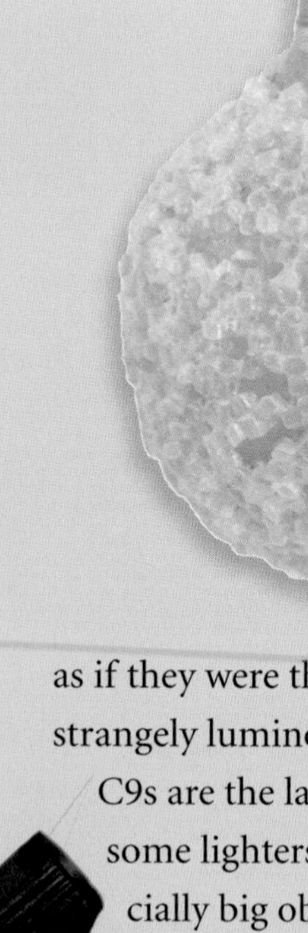

Once you figure out what you want your display to look like, it's off to the hardware store to buy the necessary parts. And oh, what a strange and wonderful trip it can be. The people who make and sell lights provide enough bulbs and accessories to confuse even the shrewdest lights enthusiast.

The first step for smart shopping is knowing about the bulbs themselves. When most people envision the old-fashioned lights that they saw when Mom and Dad took them to see the neighborhood displays, they're probably thinking of C9s and C7s. These lamps have long, tapered bulbs shaped a little like flames, or maybe mutant avocados, and are about the size of the bulbs that go into night lights.

The main difference between C7s and C9s is that the latter are bigger. Depending on which bulb manufacturer you consult, a C9 bulb can run up to 2¾ inches tall, while a C7 bulb can get as short as 1½ inches. For the exhibitionists among us, there are even bulbs that are shaped like C7s and C9s but are much bigger — a solid 11 inches tall. You can hang these monsters on trees or stake them into the ground as if they were themselves short (if strangely luminous) trees.

C9s are the lamp of choice among some lighters for decorating especially big objects. The website of Christmas Pro Shop recommends using them for rooflines, gables, ground lighting, large trees, and the outlines of buildings or other large objects.

If you're planning anything especially elaborate, you're in luck: C9s and C7s come preinstalled on spools of wire up to 1,000 feet long. (Just make sure your electrical system can handle them!)

One problem with C7 and C9 lights, especially the C9s, is that they devour power. C9 bulbs use seven to ten watts of electricity each, while C7s take five to seven watts each. "If you have a strand of 50 five-watt bulbs, the strand consumes 250 watts," says the website How Stuff Works. "Consider that most people need [at least] five or ten strands to do a house, and you are talking about a lot of power." A lot, indeed: If you power more

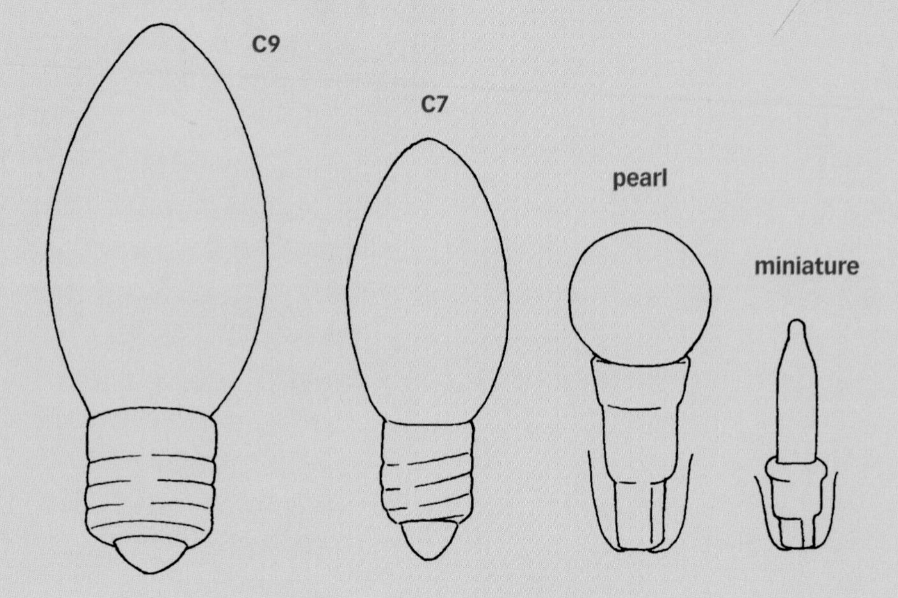

than three strands of C9s from a traditional outlet, you risk blowing a fuse. And since the power goes into burning a filament until it glows white-hot, fifty C7s can generate as much warmth as a small space heater, and C9s even more.

To avoid this problem, you can buy mini-lights. Miniature light bulbs, introduced in the 1970s, need only ten to thirty percent of the power that C7s and C9s use. These tiny creatures are cylindrical tubes that taper to a point, like candles. Christmas Pro Shop recommends them for decorating shrubs, small trees, windows, wreaths, garlands, and the outlines of buildings or objects.

Even smaller than mini-lights are tiny devils that go by various names —micro-lights, ultra-small lights, rice lights, and sometimes twinkle lights — but all have one thing in common: They're teeny, no more than a tenth of an inch or about the size of a grain of rice.

"Twinkle lights are most effective when purchased in a single color, such as white or blue," reports journalist J. Scott Wilson, whose syndicated column "The Weird Chronicles" covers a range of strange and quirky things. "If you want to run lights through a hedge or around a tree trunk, the multicolored twinkle lights lose their impact." They're so small that some companies consider them "specialty lights," a category reserved for the freakish and faddish.

Among the most popular specialty lights of our times are pearl lights. They do look a little like pearls, if pearls came in red, yellow, green, blue, and other brilliant hues. Manufacturers and retailers like to call these perfect spheres "elegant" and "simple." They somewhat resemble old-style theater footlights, a convenient similarity if you want to make your displays look like stage sets with Santas and snowmen as the actors.

Or the lights themselves can be Santas and snowmen — or almost anything else. You've probably seen bulbs shaped like cartoon characters or chili peppers, but that's *so* twentieth century. These days, you can find lights with the forms and colors of tikis, candy corn, zebras, firemen's helmets, parrots, hot dogs, lobsters, Pittsburgh Steelers helmets, dogs with fire hydrants, and just about anything else you can think of.

Possibly the oddest specialty lights are the Festive Shotgun Shells Holiday Lights from Kevin's Fine Outdoor Gear and Apparel of Tallahassee, Florida. Humorist Dave Barry has described them thusly: "Nothing says 'Ho, ho, ho' like these festive holiday lights, which are made from used shotgun shells. At least we hope they are used. We don't like to think about what would happen if you plugged these babies in and they turned out to be loaded."

SPECIALTY BULBS

Specialty bulbs come in all shapes and flavors. **(1)** Large Asian-style lanterns work well outdoors. **(2)** Tropical fruit bulbs make a *unique* — that is, tacky or chic, depending on your taste — indoor Christmas tree.

Arrays of Light

Once you know what kind of bulbs you want, you have to figure out how you want to deploy them. Light arrays come in all kinds of strands, ropes, nets, and other forms.

Strands

The most common and simple version is the strand. With wires covered in insulation that is usually green (to blend into shrubbery), these creatures are pretty simple. However, do not confuse them with the strings of lights used to decorate indoor Christmas trees; any strand of lights you use outdoors should be rated specifically for outdoor use.

Some strands come with a controller. The controller can turn the lights on and off in patterns that make the lights seem to run down the strand — called "chasing" in the lights game. It can also set up a variety of flashes and electric dances.

Icicle lights: fad or phenomenon?

Icicles

Strands are the most traditional of lights arrays. Newer to the game, having gained popularity only in the 1990s, are icicle lights. These small strands of bulbs are designed to hang from gutters and eaves. They come in various uneven lengths, just like actual frozen-water icicles.

Once (and sometimes still) dismissed as a fad, icicle lights have hung on — literally. As columnist J. Scott Wilson has said, "They are supposed to look like icicles and thus should be hung where you might possibly *find* an icicle." Icicle lights are meant to dangle, so it's not safe to wrap them tightly around objects.

There's another reason to use icicles selectively. "Icicle lights have more lights per linear foot than regular light strands and use more energy," says a set of guidelines from The Alliance to Save Energy, a group of business, government, environmental, and consumer leaders that promotes energy efficiency. In other words, too many icicle lights in December can bring on a nasty electric bill in January.

Rope lights come in small coils of tubing.

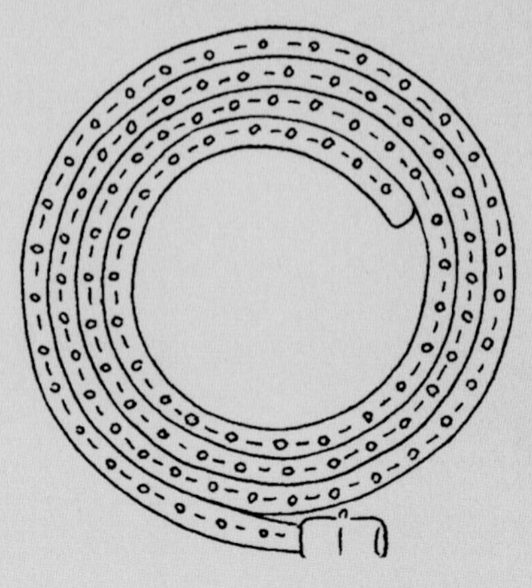

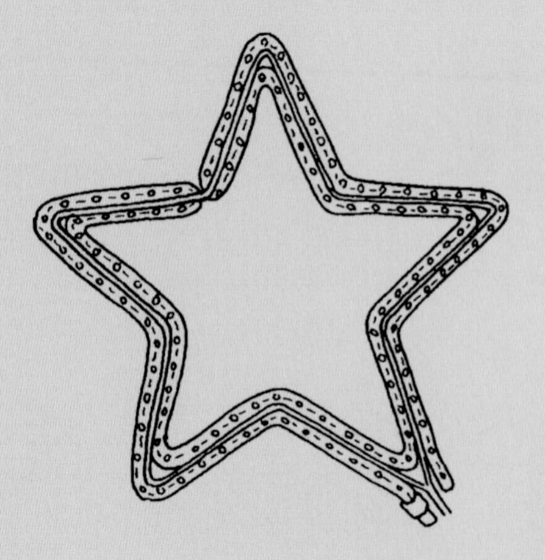

You can bend the tubing to create just about any shape imaginable.

Ropes

If you're worried that an electric spark from icicles or strands might ignite your lawn, tree, or home, one solution is rope light: a strand of lights inside a flexible, translucent plastic tube, which neatly muffles any heat or sparks. The tube also repels water, a useful trait for anything that deals with electricity; boat owners often use rope lights to decorate their ships. And ropes can look very modern;

gardening colunist Kathy Van Mullekom has noted that rope lights work well "for the contemporary character . . . to give any architectural feature a streamlined look."

Nets

But let's say that you just want to cover a lot of area fast. In that case, you might try net lights. Net lights are just that — a net of lights, with bulbs poking up at every juncture where the net's strands overlap.

You can drape net lights like a blanket over bushes, trees, cars, or any number of other objects. Need to light up an area eight feet square with nearly 300 bulbs? No problem. Want to make an illuminated flag? Start changing the bulbs on the net until you get the pattern that you want.

Light Sculptures

If changing the bulbs on a net is too much trouble, you can always buy net lights pre-bulbed with a flag pattern. In fact, many companies will be happy to sell you lights pre-arranged in the shape of flags, Santas, trees, reindeer, tree ornaments, and all sorts of other things. You can find a crescent moon in a sleepy-time stocking cap, Christmas trees playing guitars and saxophones, a polar bear munching a candy cane, deer kissing each other, toy soldiers firing cannons, a cactus topped by a five-pointed star, and penguins standing next to igloos or perching on ice floes. And Santas, lots and lots of Santas: Santa driving a Corvette or a '57 Chevy, Santa waving from a helicopter, Santa dunking a basketball, Santa golfing (apparently a very popular design), and an upended half-Santa with his rear end facing skyward and legs in mid-kick — perfect for the top of one's chimney.

If you want to go big, you can buy a drive-through guard house and other giant images drawn in rows of bulbs.

Net lights, offering symmetrical, even coverage, are a perfectionist's dream.

Want a snowflake four feet in diameter? No problem for anyone with about $150. A seven-foot palm tree for your Nativity scene, or just to add a tropical touch to your snowy winter? Sure, for $120 plus tax and shipping. In fact, if you're willing to put out a few hundred bucks, you can get an entire Christmas train, flights of angels, whole Christmas villages, or anything else that imagination can conjure.

The Savvy Shopper

Obviously, not every bulb is suited for every purpose. Over and over, experts on the subject give the same advice when it comes to shopping for holiday lights.

Check the website of the United States Consumer Products Safety Commission (www.cpsc.gov) for a list of lights recalls. In 2002, for instance, the CPSC asked NBG International, Flora-Lite Company, Winstar International, and other lighting companies to recall their light strands. The reasons included wires that could cause electric shocks and plugs that wouldn't stay securely in sockets. The CPSC also asked Homemaster Inc. to recall its Outdoor Lighting Timers because of flawed wiring.

When you go shopping for new lights, take a list of the recalled lights with you. And if the lights stored in your attic have been recalled, trash them.

Look on the packaging of all new lights for the UL seal. Like extension cords, lights should be certified by Underwriters Laboratories.

Make sure that the lights are designed to work where you want them to. Most light sets are rated for outdoor or indoor use. If you use outdoor lights indoors, or vice versa, you could be inviting fire, electric shock, or power failure.

To make sure they're in good working order, check the lights as soon as possible after you've brought them home. Examine them for cracked sockets, exposed wires, and loose connections. Plug them in and see if they light up, if their controllers make the lights flash as they should, and so on. Check each light strand for overheating by setting it on a nonflammable surface and plugging it in for about 15 minutes. If anything starts to smoke or melt, get rid of the strand.

If you've bought a light set that does not work properly, don't try to fix it. Instead, take it back to the store where you purchased it for a refund or exchange.

On the Cheap

If you're worried that your display might cost a lot of money to light, you don't have to worry — at least, not much. The equipment may get costly, but the power supply doesn't have to. There are a number of ways to keep your electricity costs down.

First, be sure to put your lights on a timer so that they turn off automatically rather than burn all night.

Second, install low-wattage bulbs. This doesn't necessarily equate to dimming down your display. LED lights are a bright low-power option. Another possibility is fiber-optic lights. These thin, flexible, extremely low-watt strands of glass carry light of any color and are especially bright at the tips. You can buy fiber-optic Christmas trees, Santas, snowmen, angels, and other symbols of the season. As of this writing, though, it seems that virtually no one has stuffed a bundle of fiber-optic strands into a receptacle that looks like a C7, a mini-light or any other conventional holiday lamp. Maybe next year.

As a last resort, you can move. There's a reason why Chuck Smith can put up more than 100,000 lights on his PlanetChristmas display and all of Gatlinburg can light up: They're in Tennessee, which has some of the lowest power rates in the country. "In Knoxville, for example, a display on the order of . . . 100 strings each with 100 miniature lights (41 watts per string), one 100-watt Santa figure and a 450-watt set of floodlights illuminating a nativity scene . . . would generate added costs of $63. That's assuming the lights (totaling 4,650 watts) are left on seven hours per day for 30 days," says a December 2002 press release from the United States Department of Energy's Oak Ridge National Laboratory. "A New Yorker with the same display would be paying an extra $136 to spread holiday cheer, while a jolly homeowner in Hawaii would see an extra $160 on his or her electric bill."

To allow consumers a more thorough comparison, the lab projects the costs for a display of ten light strands, each with 100 miniature lights, plus one 100-watt lighted Santa (510 watts total), for regions across the continent, broken down by total cost and also cost per kilowatt-hour (kwh). The results are posted at right.

COMPARING THE COSTS OF POWER

- East South Central (Alabama, Kentucky, Mississippi, and Tennessee): $12.96 (6.43 cents per kwh)
- West North Central (Iowa, Kansas, Minnesota, Missouri, Nebraska, North Dakota, and South Dakota): $14.82 (7.35 cents per kwh)
- Mountain (Arizona, Colorado, Idaho, Montana, Nevada, New Mexico, Utah, and Wyoming): $14.96 (7.42 cents per kwh)
- South Atlantic (Delaware, District of Colombia, Florida, Georgia, Maryland, North Carolina, South Carolina, Virginia, and West Virginia): $15.52 (7.70 cents per kwh)
- West South Central (Arkansas, Louisiana, Oklahoma, and Texas): $15.66 (7.77 cents per kwh)
- East North Central (Illinois, Indiana, Michigan, Ohio, and Wisconsin): $16.57 (8.22 cents per kwh)
- Pacific Contiguous (California, Oregon, and Washington): $17.60 (8.73 cents per kwh)
- New England (Connecticut, Maine, Massachusetts, New Hampshire, Rhode Island, and Vermont): $22.52 (11.17 cents per kwh)
- Middle Atlantic (New Jersey, New York, and Pennsylvania): $22.96 (11.39 cents per kwh)
- Pacific Noncontiguous (Alaska and Hawaii): $29 (14.42 cents per kwh)

Clips Ahoy! (and Tape, Too)

All your electrical paraphernalia has to get attached to your home somehow. While you're at the hardware store picking up light strings and extension cords, you'll need to get some mounting equipment, too.

Putting up lights is a specialized job, so don't trust it to your usual fasteners. Some people punch nails, staples, screws, or hooks into their homes and hang the lights from them, but those fasteners can damage wall joints and other sensitive areas. They don't work well elsewhere, either; as home decorating expert Leland Edward Stone has written, "The roof was put there to repel water. The last thing it needs is to be poked full of nail holes." An even worse idea is to attach the light strands into your home by pounding nails and such directly through the strands. That's a fast way to damage a strand's wires, it can be a pain to remove, and it usually looks ugly.

A better (and easier) way to attach lights to your home is by covering the strands with several strong, tight layers of weatherproof electrical tape. Electrical tape is also a good tool for protecting electrical connections. Wherever anything plugs into anything else, a tight wrap of tape around the connection will hold it together and safeguard it from moisture.

Clips are useful, too. They hold lights to surfaces by applying simple, safe pressure. There are different clips for different purposes. Shingle tab clips are good for putting lights, especially the larger C7s and C9s, along a roofline. Using one tab per bulb, slip the bottom of each bulb through the tab's hole, and screw the bulb securely into its base. Once you have all of your bulbs in place, slide the tabs up under the roof shingles (with the bulbs facing away from the roof), and clip each tab to a shingle. The result: a neat, clean row of lights.

Parapet clips, which work on surfaces without shingles, don't attach lights to surfaces as shingle tabs do; they keep a row of lights facing or aiming in the same direction, while electrical tape or another adhesive holds the clips in place. C clips, so named because they're shaped like the letter C, do the same kind of job as parapet clips but are usually bigger. Gutter clips, on the other hand, are molded to fit rain gutters; they don't slide in like shingle tabs but snap into place. And brick clips attach lights to bricks. Unlike other clips, which are made of plastic, a brick clip is made of metal. It clings to a brick wall by grabbing the top and bottom edges of an individual brick, which usually poke out beyond the surrounding mortar.

There are many other kinds of clips as well. Tree clips attach lights to trees (well, duh); mini-clips are sized for miniature lights; all-in-one clips are versatile enough to handle lights of different sizes and can fit onto shingles or gutters; and so on.

Electrical Tape

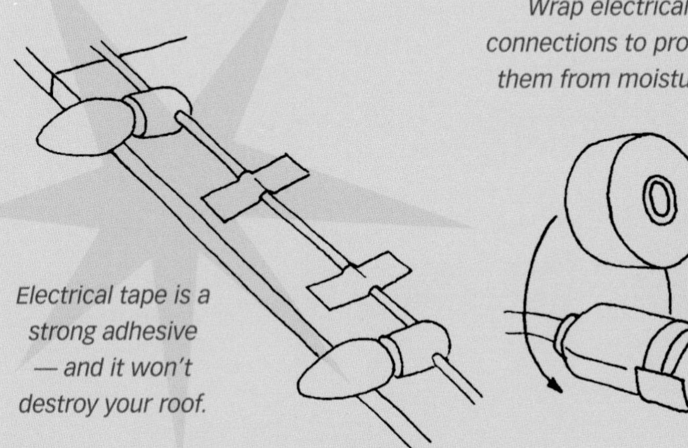

Wrap electrical connections to protect them from moisture.

Electrical tape is a strong adhesive — and it won't destroy your roof.

C Clip

Multipurpose C clips can be fastened to a variety of surfaces.

C clip

Gutter Clip (Strands)

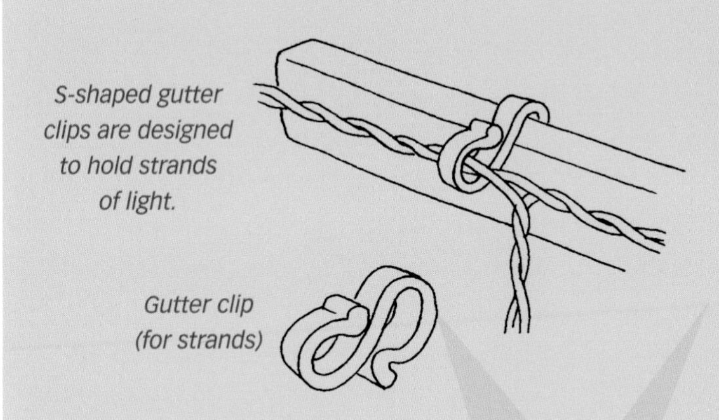

S-shaped gutter clips are designed to hold strands of light.

Gutter clip (for strands)

Gutter Clip (Bulbs)

Upright gutter clips are designed to hold individual bulbs.

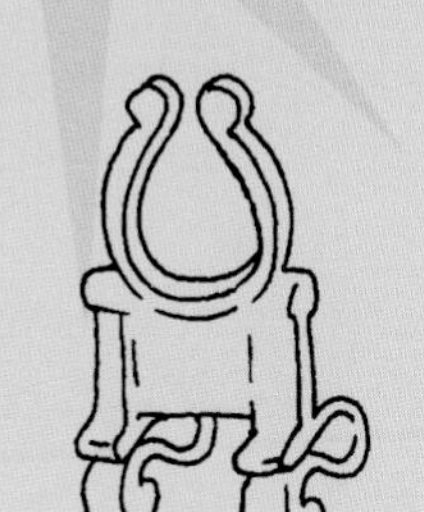

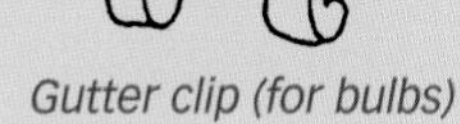

Gutter clip (for bulbs)

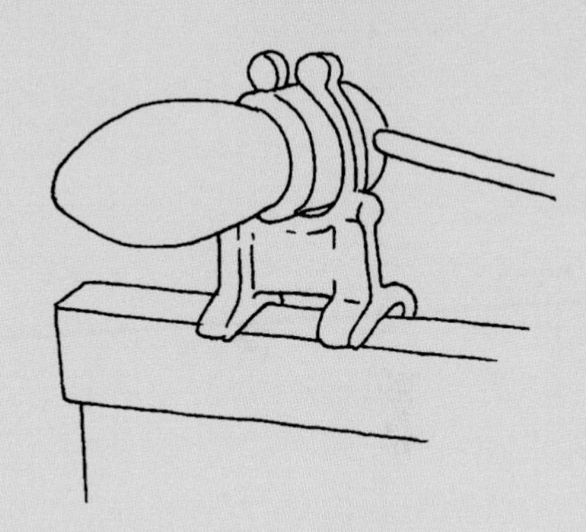

Shingle Tab Clip

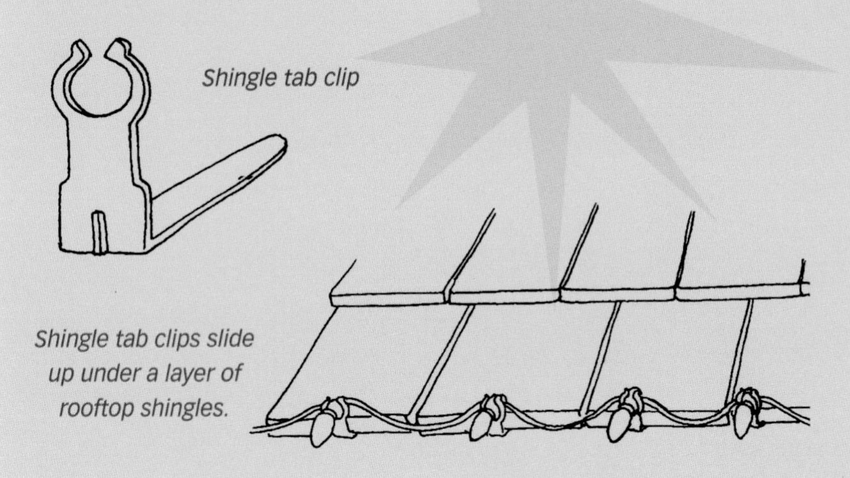

Shingle tab clip

Shingle tab clips slide up under a layer of rooftop shingles.

Brick Clip

Brick clip

The brick clip is designed to span a single brick, clinging to the wall like a climber to a cliff.

Tree Topping

Before you put lights in that grand old oak gracing your front yard, remember that no more than three strands of lights (or however many are recommended by the strands' manufacturer) should be strung together. Giving a tree mass coverage of lights, then, will require many bunches of strands, each of which have to plug into an outlet. If a tree is far from your outlets, you'll have to hide the extension cords.

People who decorate lots of really tall trees sometimes rent a bucket truck, also known as a lift truck. This machine does what its name implies: The driver parks the vehicle, enters a bucket big enough for a human being and his lights, and by manipulating the controls raises the bucket as high as he needs to go.

Before you rent a bucket lift truck, learn how to run it. "Only trained persons shall operate an aerial lift," says rule 1910.67(c)(2)(ii) of the United States Occupational Safety and Health Administration. According to an article in *Communications Technology*, a magazine for (among others) people who string wires in high places, "The aerial lift truck, more commonly called a bucket truck, is by far the most complex form of aerial transportation . . . Sometimes, just getting a bucket truck to the work area is a job in itself. An average bucket truck weighs 10,000 pounds and cannot stop on a dime. This is why the trucks are notorious for hitting other vehicles in rear-impact accidents." Then there's the problem of raising the bucket too fast and ripping through a tree's upper branches. Consequently, you should look up "Truck Driving Instruction" in your local yellow pages and find out about classes in operating bucket lift trucks.

On the other hand, you might get lucky and find a bucket truck for the asking. For years, brothers Brent and Aaron Sharp of Savannah, Georgia, have put up more than 30,000 lights on their family home. "We asked the local fire department to helps us out by using their bucket truck to put the lights in the trees in our front yard," Brent says. "The fire fighters were volunteers, so this was used as practice with the bucket truck."

If renting a bucket truck is out of the question, you have a few other options.

Homegrown Methods

Some people simply toss strands of lights into trees. This method doesn't let you control where the strands go, but it can be a lot of fun. However, unless you have a strong arm or a short tree, you may not be able to reach the highest branches.

For more control and greater reaching power, get a long wooden pole and attach a small hook to one end. Drape a string of lights over the hook and extend the pole over one of the tree's branches. Turn the pole until the strand slips off of the hook and onto the branch, dangling like a kite string. If possible, grab the dangling end of the strand with the hook and wrap the strand around the branch to secure it.

While the pole method is more reliable than the toss-and-hope technique, for the most part it still lets luck and gravity determine where the lights hang. If you'd rather make these choices yourself, use a ladder to get yourself deep into the tree's foliage so you can reach the branches easily. Attach the lights to the branches with tree clips or twist ties.

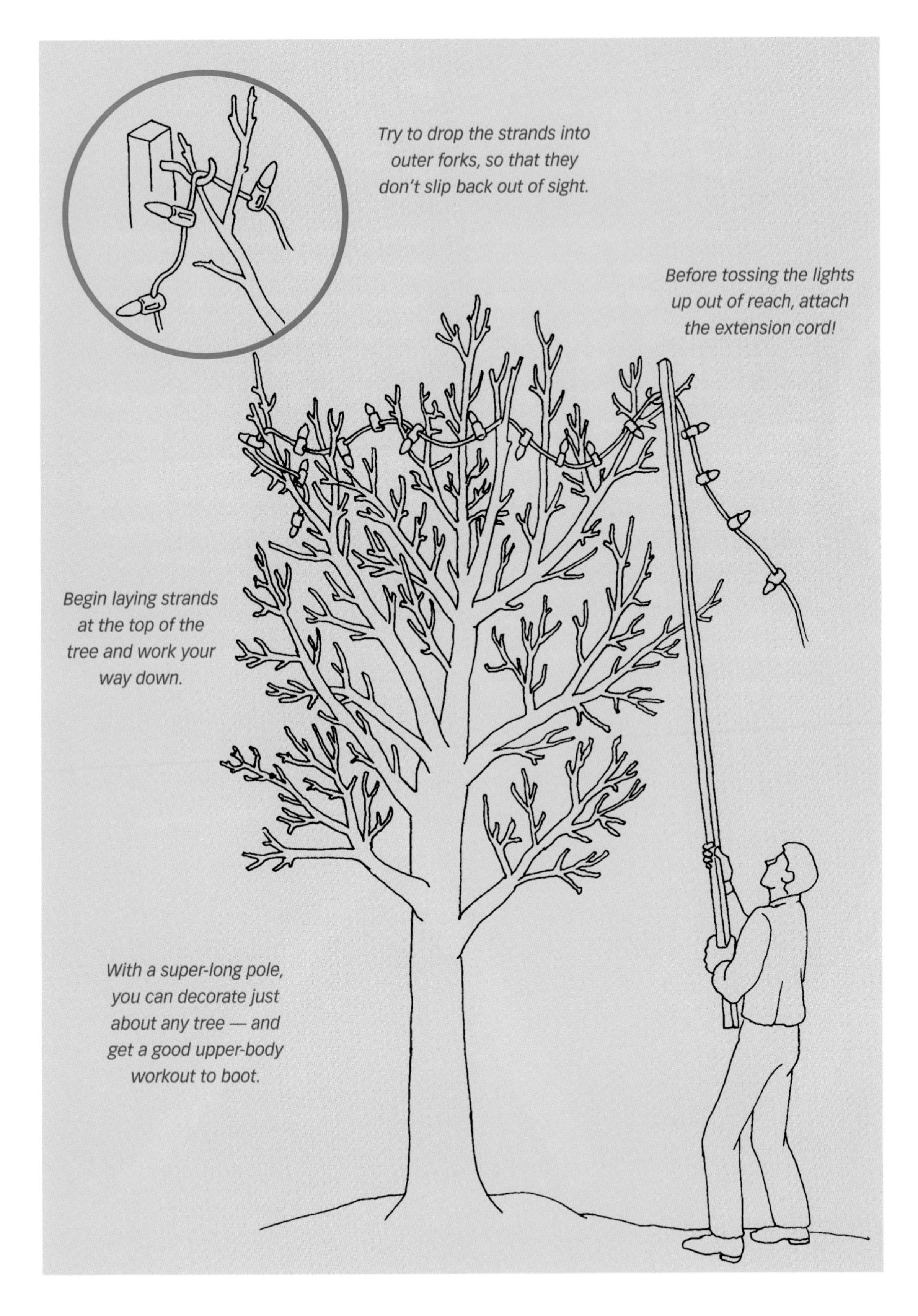

Two Lighting Techniques

There are as many ways to light trees as there are people who enjoy doing it. Simple techniques include **(1)** loosely looping lights around a tree's foliage and **(2)** tightly wrapping lights around a tree's branches and trunk.

Rooflines, Gutters, Gables, and Eaves

If you're not a professional roofer, it's safest to limit your roof lights to the eaves, gables, and other structures along the roof's edge. That way, you don't have to get on the roof itself, which can be a surpringly treacherous task, especially if the roof is particularly steep.

Attaching lights to gables, eaves, and such is fairly straightforward if you use the right clips; see pages 144–145 for more information. Your most important task is to put the lights in places that are safe. Keep all lights, cords, and other items away from metal; electricity and metal make a dangerous mix. Overhead wires, ironwork décor, and aluminum gutters or eaves are all tricky areas. Any places that get especially hot, like chimneys, are troublesome as well, because they can melt insulation.

Finally, before you lug all those lights and clips up the ladder, you'll want to make sure that the design you've planned will have the desired effect. Lay out the lights on the ground, running them parallel to the areas where you want to light them. In that way, before you hang them, you can see how they'll look in real space rather than just as a sketch on a photo.

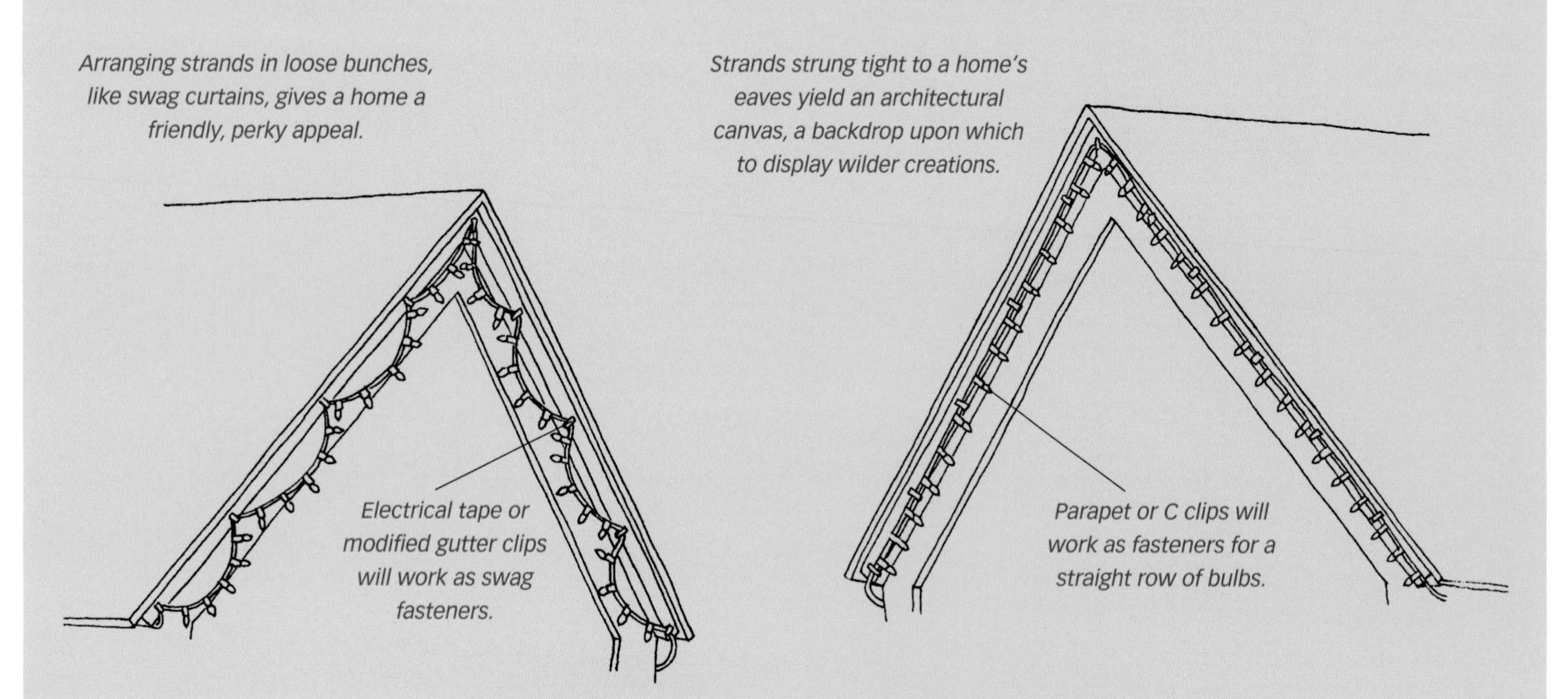

Arranging strands in loose bunches, like swag curtains, gives a home a friendly, perky appeal.

Strands strung tight to a home's eaves yield an architectural canvas, a backdrop upon which to display wilder creations.

Windows and Doors

Bright lights lining roofs and wrapping around trees attract a visitor's eye to the outskirts of your property. To pull attention toward the center of things — inviting the visitor into your home, so to speak — light up your doors and windows.

To begin, a cautionary note: Don't light the doors themselves. Lights placed directly on any moving fixture may swing and bang against its surface, which can jar a connection loose or crack a bulb. Instead, attach lights above and around doors, on the cornices and casings.

Some people secure lights only at the top of a door or window and let them dangle freely. This setup can be pretty, but it's not a good idea if your area suffers strong winds. Again, you risk that banging problem.

About bulbs: Think about using minilights in doorways and windows. Big bulbs like C9s can be handsome from far off, but they may not look very elegant just inches from a visitor's nose. To make your door and window lights as attractive as possible, consider using more than one line of bulbs. A single strand around a door or window can look lonely and sad, while multiple strands can look cheerful and luxurious. Besides, a large number of lights can distract the visitor's eye from any small problems.

If you're a little sloppy in putting strands of bulbs up in trees or on rooftops, your visitors may never notice. However, lights on doorways and windows will be at your visitors' eye level. At such close range, visitors can see every unsightly strip of electrical tape or clumsily applied clip. So work carefully in these areas, being sure to arrange bulbs evenly.

You might also consider prefabricated garlands of lights. With a little diligent shopping, you can buy long garlands with bulbs entwined among fireproof artificial leaves. They look festive and Christmassy and can hide a multitude of installation sins.

No matter what you use, remember safety. If you hang multiple strands, keep them from touching each other. In particular, stagger hot components such as sockets and bulbs to keep them out of each other's way.

Pictures Perfect

In order to preserve the gorgeousness of your display — and to have a record of it to help you duplicate it next year — you'll want to take pictures of it at full blast. But getting photos of lights at night isn't always easy. Herewith, some advice.

- Don't wait for the night to get completely black. Dusk is a great time to take photos of holiday lights. The lights show up almost as well around sunset as they do at midnight, and as photo expert Lynne Eodice has written, "Colorful skies and Christmas lights can result in some beautiful holiday images."
- To capture the lights best, use fast film stock. ISO 800 seems to work best. (ISO, by the way, stands for International Standards Organization, a group that sets film speeds and other measurements.)
- Use a tripod rather than just your own hands. A hand shivering in the winter cold doesn't take the steadiest pictures. Besides, according to the authoritative New York Institute of Photography (NYIP), "You're probably going to need a very slow shutter speed. This means you should mount your camera on a solid unmoving surface to avoid camera-shake."
- Leave your strobe light at home. If you use fast film and a slow shutter, the holiday lights themselves should provide all the illumination that your camera needs.
- Keep street lamps and other sources of light out of the picture. Their glow on film may interfere with the glow from the C7s, LEDs, and icicle lights.
- For truly dramatic photos, take close-up shots. Focusing in on a subject lends it dramatic power, removes clutter from the surroundings, and, best of all, is a hassle-free way to get high-quality photos.
- To capture movement in an animated display, first get a sense of its timing, and then shoot just slightly in advance of the moment you want to capture. Remember: The depression of the "shoot" button and the closure of the shutter is not instantaneous. Of course, if you have a digital camera, this problem will become moot — you can simply save the appropriate frame and discard the others.
- Take plenty of pictures. Development costs are relatively low these days, and with every shot you take, you increase your chances of getting that picture-perfect photograph.
- The cold and damp of winter can be tough on cameras. Until you're ready to shoot, keep your camera handy but in someplace snug, like a purse or a car's glove box.

Going to Ground

If you have a fear of heights and would prefer not to dangle from ladders near roofs, trees, and other high places, the ground is always waiting for you. Driveways, walkways, and flower beds look festive when lit and can serve as a horizontal canvas for renderings of whatever images or patterns complement your vertical display.

Unfortunately, the ground tends to accumulate snow, dew, and other kinds of moisture. Unless you want to electrocute trespassers, it's best to keep your lights away from anything soggy.

The solution is to keep the lights and cords above ground. One tool for this job is the humble garden stake. This isn't a job for a Popsicle stick marked "radishes," though. The stakes should be strong and firm enough to support the weight of lights and cords. Just clip the lights to the stakes.

Better than a garden stake, though, is a universal light stake. Usually made of durable plastic, with a sharp point at the bottom to penetrate the ground and hooks or tabs at the top to hold the lights, a universal stake can handle C7s, C9s, and miniature lights. Some are even designed to hold longs strands of rope light.

Some Christmas lights companies combine lights and stakes in one pre-fab unit. Firms like Christmas Lights, Etc., for example, offer short, bulb-bedecked, Christmas tree stakes that "can be driven into the ground on either side of the walkway to create a welcoming aisle of greenery," according to the company's advertising.

Light stakes are designed to hold the bulbs of strands in strict order, whether upright or horizontal.

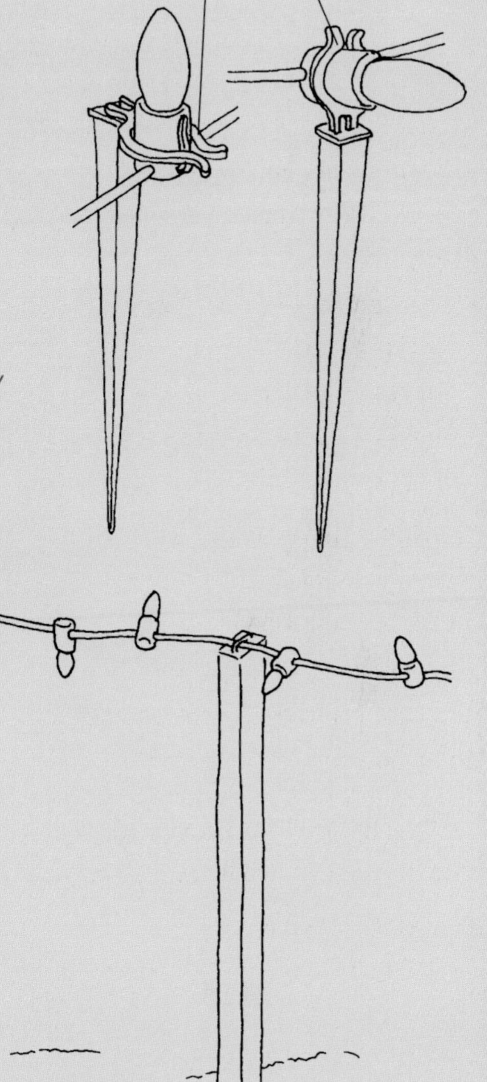

Traditional wooden garden stakes will hold strands of lights in will-nilly arrangements — charming in their own right, but certainly casual.

Archery

An upside-down U of lights over a driveway or walkway — or, even better, a row of arches creating a tunnel of light — is a handsome touch that can set your home apart from others in the neighborhood.

If your home doesn't come already equipped with arches, you'll need to build them. As with anything else in the lights game, measure and design carefully.

Make the arch out of something strong but pliable. A number of lights enthusiasts use flexible PVC tubing, which you can get at any well-stocked hardware store. PVC — properly known as polyvinyl chloride — is a white plastic often formed into pipes for outdoor plumbing. It comes in both rigid and

flexible versions; to make an arch, it's best to get flexible Schedule 40 pipe. A schedule, in piping jargon, is a measure of the width of the pipe's wall. Schedule 40 is a fairly standard width.

The pipe's overall thickness or diameter should run from 1 to 2 inches. The taller your arch, the thicker the pipe should be. An arch over a driveway, for instance, should be thicker than an arch over a walkway.

Bend each length of PVC piping into an arch shape. Make sure that the arch's top is a smooth, symmetrical curve and that both walls are the same length.

If you're going to erect the arch on a lawn or some other soft surface, you can anchor it by burying its ends in the ground. To steady the pipe, you can use two strong metal rods, preferably steel. Each rod should be thick enough to fit snugly inside the pipe and at least twelve inches long. The bigger the arch, the longer the rods should be.

Determine the spots where the arch's arms will stand, and insert the steel rods into the ground at those spots. To push the rods down, you may need to hit them with a hammer. Push them in as deep as you can, provided that you can then get them out, which you'll do next. The result: two nice holes in the ground.

Insert the rods halfway into the PVC piping, and then insert the piping, rods and all, into the predug holes. If all is well, the ground will hold the arch firmly in place. If the arch arms feel loose in their holes, pack some dirt around them to hold them in place.

If you plan to set the arch on a hard surface, like a paved driveway — or if you just don't want to punch holes in your front lawn — you'll need an aboveground anchor. You might, for instance, plunge the ends of the arch into planters or flower pots tightly packed with dirt or rocks. You might also slide the ends of the arch into a patio-umbrella stand: a heavy metallic base with a tube projecting upward. The tube, which should have a handle that you can turn to to make it smaller or bigger, must become big enough to hold your PVC piping.

Once the arch is up, attach the lights. You can wind strings of lights around the arch as if you were braiding it, run the lights straight along the structure to outline it, or pick some other pattern that tickles your fancy. In any case, secure the lights to the arch with electrical tape or whatever clips will get the job done. If possible, attach the lights so that the bulbs point away from the arch, rather than lying against it.

Now, you're done — except that you're not, really. As with every other kind of light setup, you should check the arch occasionally to make sure that it's still firmly in place. Storms, accident-prone children, and other natural forces can topple an arch or even a series of arches like a row of dominoes.

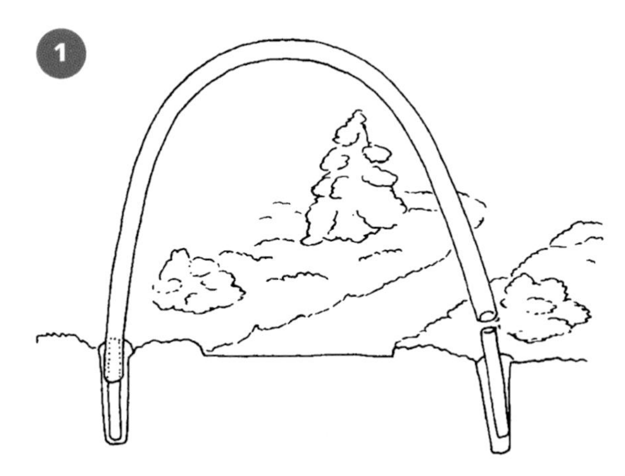

Anchoring an Arch

You can anchor your arch either aboveground or belowground. **Belowground (1):** Secure the pipe ends over steel bars sunk in the ground. **Aboveground (2):** Slip the pipe ends into or over an umbrella-stand base or into heavy planters.

Wooden Cut-Outs

Painted wooden cut-outs can stand on their own as holiday yard art, or you can string lights on them to augment your nighttime lighting event. In any case, they are a simple craft project that even the artistically challenged can undertake.

All you'll need for this project is a large sheet of plywood, a pencil, a jigsaw, a drill (if you intend to light your cut-out), exterior-grade paint, several paintbrushes, and some scrap wood.

The first step in making a wooden cut-out is, obviously, deciding on a pattern. If you're reasonably good at drafting, you can trace your design right onto a large sheet of plywood. If you want to make more than one of a particular cut-out, trace the pattern onto a large sheet of cardboard, which you can then cut out and use as a template.

If your drafting skills leave something to be desired, try drawing your pattern in miniature on a piece of graph paper. (Working small may allow you to copy a pattern from another source, such as a kid's coloring book.) Number the squares of the first row and letter the squares of the first column, as if the graph were a map. Draw a similar graph on the sheet of plywood, making each square considerably larger. Number and letter the larger squares to match the setup on the graph paper. Then transfer the design from the graph paper to the plywood, working square by square.

You'll find that it's easier to draw on a large scale when you can focus on just

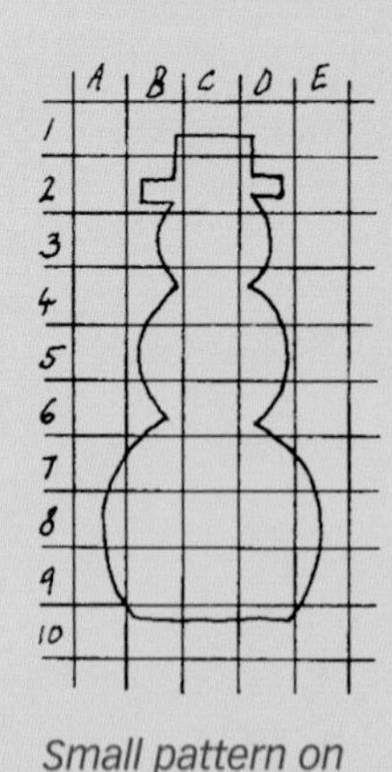

Small pattern on small graph paper.

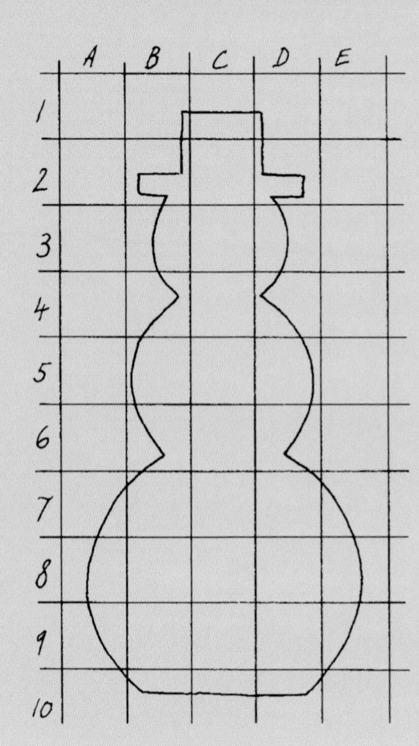

Full-size pattern on a large graph

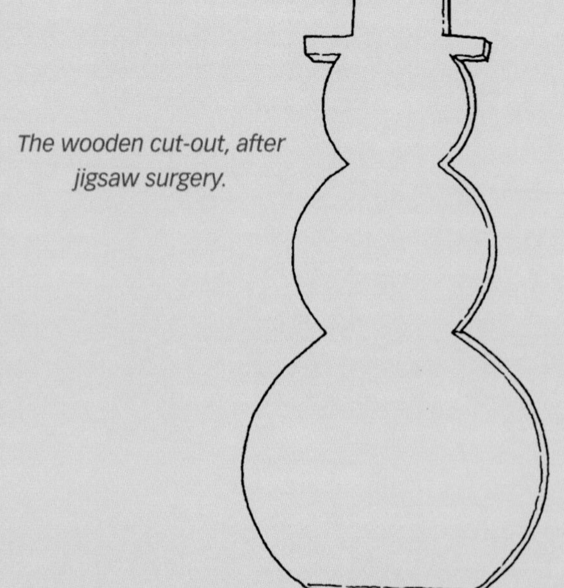

The wooden cut-out, after jigsaw surgery.

one small piece of the overall pattern at a time. You may find it easiest to tranfer any straight lines first, leaving curves for last.

Once your design is laid out on the plywood or cardboard, you're practically done. Use the jigsaw to cut around the outline of the pattern and to cut out any holes within its boundaries. Do your best to avoid leaving jagged or ragged edges, which could result in painful splinters.

If you want your cut-out to be seen at night, you have two options. First, you can spotlight it with floodlights. This setup works best if you're intending to give the cut-out an elaborate or lifelike paint job. If you can't be bothered with that sort of intricacy, you can simply string lights around the outline of the cut-out.

If you're going to wire your cut-out, find light strands with tapered bulbs, like the one shown below. Measure the diameter of the bulb socket, where it joins the strand, and drill holes that same size through the cut-out in all the appropriate places. Keep the holes close together, so that the cut-out will glow with lights.

Use scrap wood to build a sturdy brace, like the back of an artist's easel, that will hold the cut-out upright. Secure the brace directly to the cut-out with galvanized screws.

Give the cut-out a thick coat of paint. Remember that its true moments of glory will come at night; use bright paints whenever possible. After the paint has dried, push the bulbs of your light strands, if you're using them, through the predrilled holes.

Then head outdoors to put your new display in place.

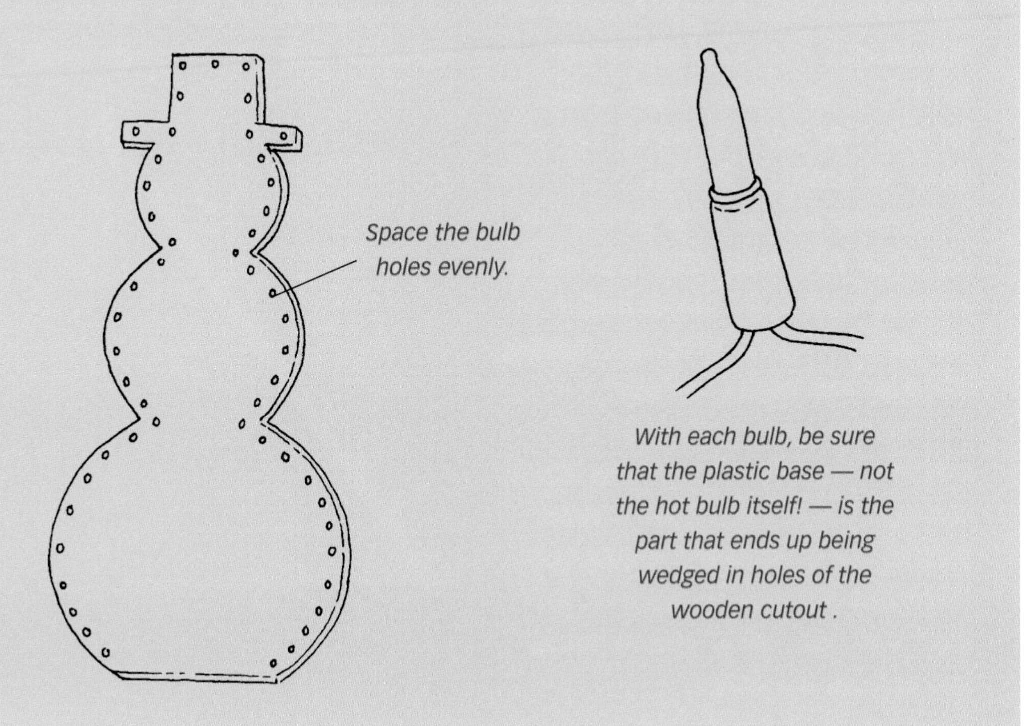

With each bulb, be sure that the plastic base — not the hot bulb itself! — is the part that ends up being wedged in holes of the wooden cutout .

LIGHTING WIRE FORMS

Holiday-themed wire forms can be found at most hardware stores and larger retailers during the holiday season. Some are prestrung with lights; others are simple frameworks upon which to express your lighting creativity. Among the most common forms are **(1)** Santa's sleigh and **(2)** reindeer (grazing, prancing, or simply staring off into the distance).

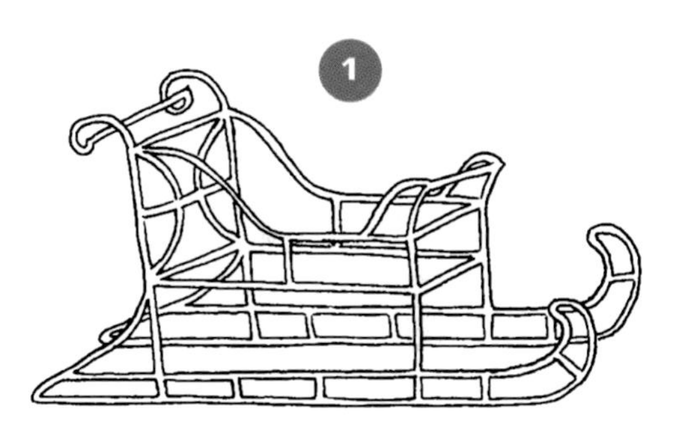

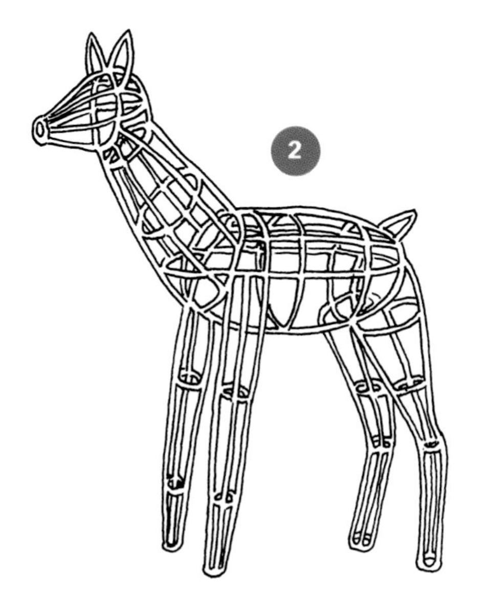

Holiday Pole-Trees

If you want a Christmas tree in your yard but don't want to buy the real thing, you can make a Maypole-esque tree of lights — a tall cone of light strands, with a pole in the middle holding it up.

The tree should stand on a flat surface — for instance, a front lawn. Draw a circle on the surface where you want the tree to stand, and mark the spot in the circle's center. The circle marks the spot where you'll anchor the lights to the ground; the center spot is where the tree's "trunk" will stand.

Now you're ready to determine how many feet of light strands you'll need to build the tree. Think of the tree as a set of right triangles projecting outward from the pole. Each triangle has a vertical side (the pole); a horizontal side (the ground); and a diagonal side (the light strand).

Remember the Pythagorean theorem: $a^2 + b^2 = c^2$. The length of the vertical side, squared, plus the length of the horizontal side, squared, equals the length of the diagonal, squared. So if the pole is 12 feet tall, and the distance from the pole to the circle is 5 feet, you do a little calculation: 12 squared is 144; 5 squared is 25; 144 plus 25 is 169. Since 169 is 13 squared, each "branch" of the tree will require 13 feet of lights.

For your convenience, there's a table of useful lengths on the facing page.

About the pole: Its exact dimensions can vary, but it should be hard, thick, and strong enough to support dozens of light strands. Drive a nail into its top; you'll wrap the strands of light around the nail. If the pole is metal, use clips to attach the strands to the pole.

To anchor the pole in the ground, you can secure it in a stable, heavy base like an umbrella stand or dirt-packed planter, or you can bury one end of the pole, holding it in place with rocks if necessary.

If the pole doesn't stand fully secure even after you anchor it, purchase sturdy, thin rope or wire and connect it tautly from the top of the pole to at least three immovable points at ground level. You don't want your tree of lights wobbling and toppling in a storm.

After you plant the pole, string the light strands, running them from the premarked circle to the top of the pole and back down to the circle again.

The tree of lights provides a lot of room for creativity. If you're feeling patriotic, you can set up the bulbs so that the top third of the tree is red, the middle third is white, and the bottom is blue. By coordinating the lights' control boxes, you can make each strand's lights chase upward from the tree's bottom so that all the bursts of light hit the top at the same time. More than one lights enthusiast has even attached the strands and pole to a platform and added a motor so that the whole apparatus turns like a merry-go-round.

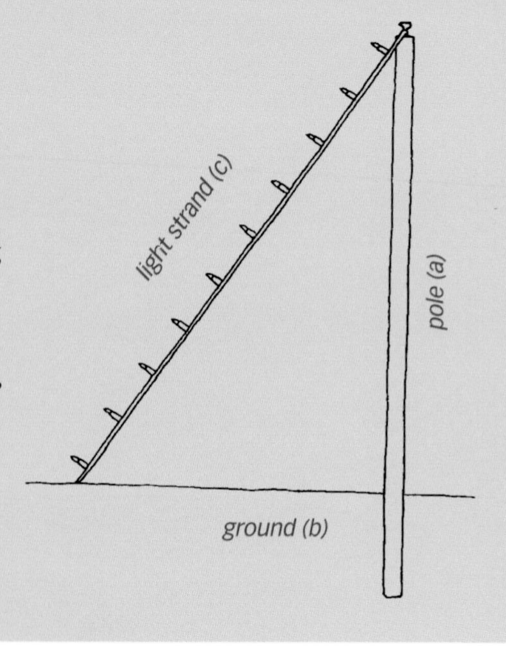

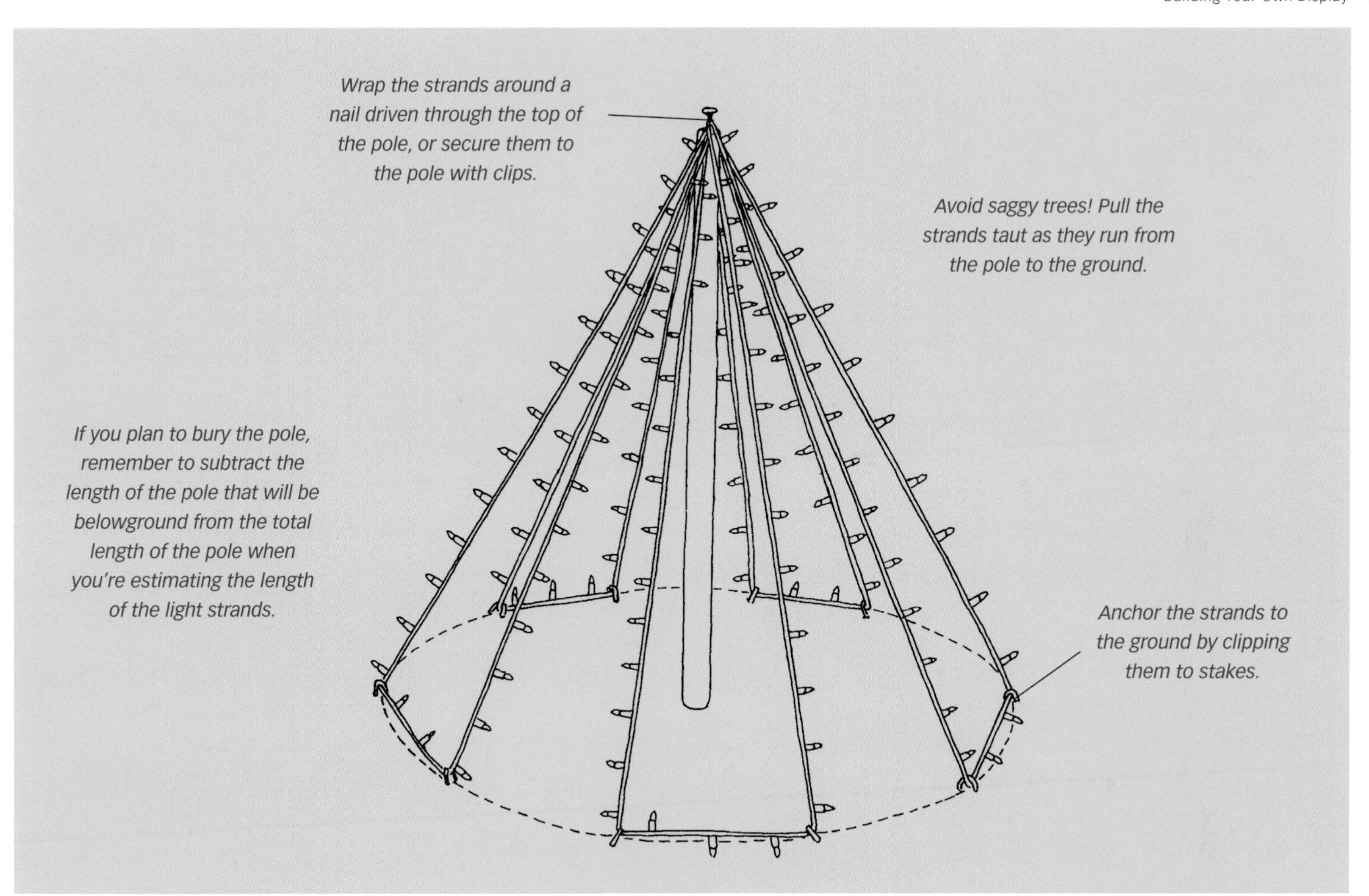

RADIUS OF CIRCLE (from pole base to circle)	**LENGTH OF POLE** (aboveground)	**LENGTH OF LIGHT STRAND** (from top of pole to circle on ground)
12 feet	5 feet	13 feet
15 feet	8 feet	17 feet
24 feet	7 feet	25 feet
35 feet	12 feet	37 feet
40 feet	9 feet	41 feet
60 feet	11 feet	61 feet

Little Trees of Light

Imagine having 192 little two-foot trees snaking through your yard, each tree on a separate circuit and each circuit controlled by the computer. That's what wiring wizard Chuck Smith did at his setup, called PlanetChristmas. Words can't describe the scene: trees appearing to chase each other back and forth, flashing simultaneously, and even stuttering. Kids actually run down the street trying to keep up with the fast-moving bursts of light racing from tree to tree.

This project is published here courtesy of Chuck Smith. He has a great website (www.planetchristmas.com) with even more projects for lighters. But the three-dimensional trees are among his favorites. These easy-to-build items are a crowd favorite, and they're also easy to store. Chuck's instructions tell you how to build one tree. Keep repeating the process until you can't stand it anymore!

Head down to your local hobby or floral store and purchase a three-legged wireframe flower easel. These easels usually have one leg that is shorter than the other, so that the easel tips back. Use tin snips or bolt cutters to shorten the two longer legs until all three are the same length.

String together three 100-light strands with multicolored bulbs. Secure the end of the first strand to the tip of the tree with a four-inch tie wrap, preferably black. (You'll need *lots* of these tie wraps.) Wind the strand down and around the easel, making the coverage as dense as possible. Wherever the strand intersects the easel, secure it in place with a tie wrap. Continue wrapping the tree, securing the strands at strategic locations with tie wraps, until all three strands are used up.

Attach a power cord and you're done!

To make a taller three-dimensional tree, simply stack the wrapped easels. Generally they can be stacked up to four high without getting tippy.

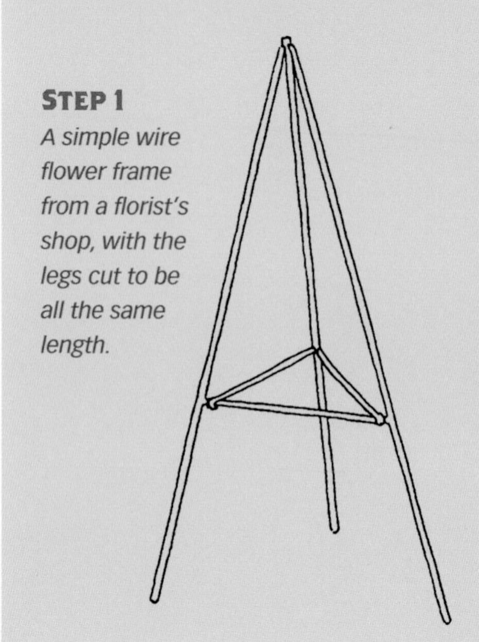

STEP 1
A simple wire flower frame from a florist's shop, with the legs cut to be all the same length.

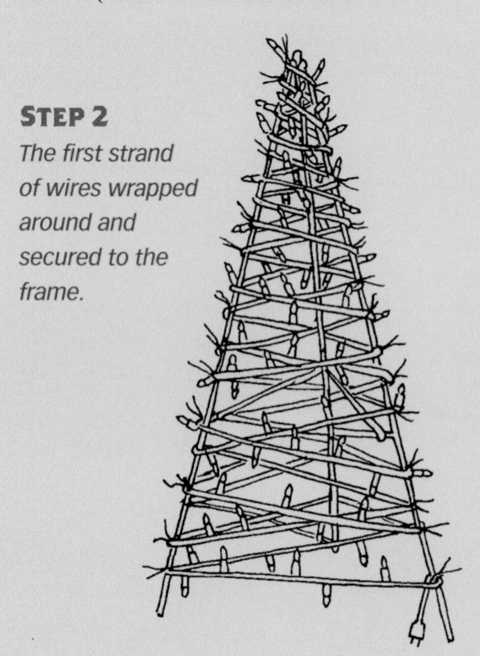

STEP 2
The first strand of wires wrapped around and secured to the frame.

STEP 3
Strands 2 and 3 piled on top of Strand 1, and the tree looking positively bushy with lights.

Digital Delirium

A rising trend in holiday lighting is automating the lights via computer. A computer can, like a timer, illuminate or douse an entire display or, like a control box, flash individual lights to create simple patterns and the illusion of movement. Unlike those machines, though, a computer can also create a variety of custom-designed animations.

Unfortunately, learning to make the computer do these tasks can daunt a newcomer, even an enthusiastic one. Take these excerpts from one instructional website: "[U]sing the parallel port is a good starting point. . . Solid state relays (SSRs) are the heart of parallel port control boxes. . . All a solid state relay really does is allow the 110V AC current to pass through when 3-8V DC is applied, and opens the AC circuit when the direct current is not present."

Unless you're an electrically minded handyman, the preceding quote probably sounded like gibberish. Let's get down to the details, then, in plain English.

Hardware (Machines)

The basic setup for computer-controlled lighting involves connecting an electronic device — generally a control box containing a set of on-off switches called relays — between the lights and the computer. The computer orders the control box to turn the lights on and off in various patterns; the control box carries out the orders.

The control box plugs into one of the computer's ports via a cable. A port is an outlet or socket, often located at the back of the computer. A cable plugs into the port, attaching the computer to a peripheral — that is, into a machine that the computer runs, like a monitor, modem, or printer. The ports that computer-lights devices use most often are the serial port and the parallel port.

The serial port, also known as the COM port (COM is short for *communication*; hardly anyone seems to know why it's capitalized), allows data to travel between the computer and a peripheral serially — that is, one bit at a time. The parallel port, also known as the printer port because it often connects the computer to a printer, allows more than one stream of data to travel at the same time. As a result, it carries data faster than the serial port.

To handle a lights display, you may have to plug more than one controller into the computer, which means using more than one port. If you've already filled most of your computer's ports with cables to various peripherals, some lights experts and lights-control manufacturers suggest running the lights on a different computer dedicated solely to the lights display. If you have an old machine that still runs decently, it may be able to do the job. To make sure, ask the makers of controllers and software (listed in this book's appendix) if their products will work with your old machine.

Many of these products go under the name X-10. Like Xerox and Band-Aid, X-10 is a brand name that many people use to describe a general category. It's a communications technology that can send orders through existing household wiring to make electrical devices turn on and off according to a schedule that you choose.

Lights enthusiasts use X-10 machines to make lights flash, chase each other, and otherwise appear to move. While you can use an X-10 timer by itself to create some basic animations, you can also send orders from your computer through an X-10 device to animate lights in much more sophisticated ways. A single X-10 device can control several groups of lights.

A standard way to use the system is to install an X-10 device called a module between your computer and whatever lights you want to control. Holiday lights enthusiasts tend to use one of two types: appliance modules and lamp modules.

An appliance module is what it sounds like: a timer that turns appliances on and off. It can, for instance, turn on an oven an hour before you get home from work and have dinner hot when you walk in the door. An appliance module is made to handle lots of electricity, since lots of electricity is what appliances use.

A lamp module can't handle as much power, but it can handle more complicated tasks. An appliance module can supply power or cut it off; a lamp module can supply it, cut it off, and adjust it. It's the machine of choice for people who like to dim and brighten their displays.

To make an X-10 module take your computer's orders, you may need a machine called an interface, plus the software to run it. An interface provides a point where one device meets another (or where hardware meets software) so that the two can communicate.

Different manufacturers issue X-10 interfaces under different names: CP290 Computer Interface, Time Commander,

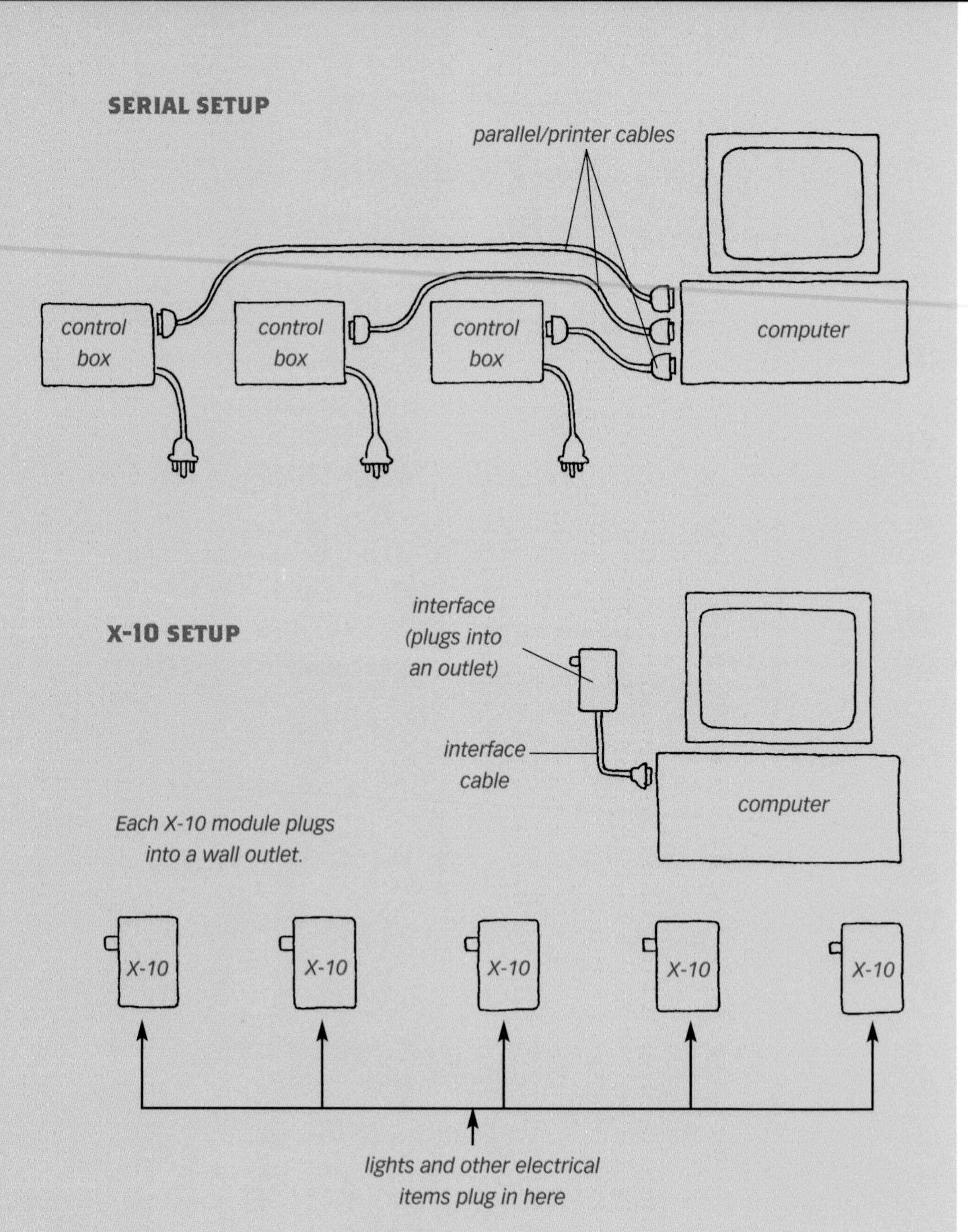

LynX-10, TW523, PL 513, CM17A Fire-Cracker, CM11A Home Director, and so on. Choosing the right interface depends on the type of computer you have, the kind of X-10 module you're using, how you plan to use it, and other factors. When in doubt, ask the people who ought to know: the ones who want to sell you the equipment. The sales force at a good hardware store, computer store, or electronics-supply website should be able to tell you which items work best with your needs and machines. You can also check in with the PlanetChristmas chat room, where your fellow holiday lighters should be happy to offer advice.

Software (Programming)

Now comes the fun part: programming your animation. As anyone who's ever done it before will know, creating a program can be immensely time-consuming, with hordes of tiny details to keep in mind. Creating a program to make thousands of lights blink on and off in patterns that imply reindeer leaping along the rooftop is not exactly the kind of chore that puts one in a happy, jolly, Christmassy state of mind.

To your rescue comes Dasher, the software that Drew Hickman created. On your screen, Dasher puts horizontal rows and vertical columns that criss-cross to form a grid of rectangles. Each row represents a piece of your display. One row might control the lights on a hedge, the next row a roofline, the next a team of six reindeer leaping into the air. For that matter, you could devote a row to each of the reindeer. The first row you'd label "Reindeer #1," the second row "Reindeer #2," and so on.

Each of the grid's columns represents a moment — let's say one second — in your display's lighting schedule. The grid's first column, therefore, would represent the sequence's first second and might be labeled "00:01.00." The next column would stand for the next second, called "00:02.00." The third column would be "00:03.00." Et cetera.

The rectangle where each row of lights overlaps with each column of time is your opportunity to give your display an order. Click on the rectangle where Reindeer #2's row overlaps 00:03.00's column, and you tell the reindeer to light up during that second. While you're at it, you can make Reindeer #1 light up during the second, fourth, and sixth seconds, or Reindeer #6 glow steadily from 00:01.00 through 00:05.00.

If you want to make the six reindeer appear to be a single reindeer heading skyward, you can have Reindeer #1 shine brightly for a second and then go black, at which point Reindeer #2 — located slightly higher in the sky — glows for a second. As Reindeer #2 goes dark, the even-higher Reindeer #3 lights up. On and on the sequence goes until the fully aloft Reindeer #6 is lit for a second, after which the cycle starts over. Voila: an animated light sequence.

Dasher and other lights programs can get pretty fancy. Among other things, they allow you to synchronize music to the lights and to store entire lighting sequences as files that run automatically.

This sort of programming doesn't come naturally to most computers. To run Dasher software, you may have to install input/output (I/O) cards inside your computer. I/O cards send various kinds of information and commands from computer to peripherals. Without the right I/O cards, you might find yourself unable to send a gorgeous set of display ideas from your computer to your lights. Unfortunately, these cards can get expensive. Consequently, a number of lighters haven't yet made the commitment to full computerization.

Back to the Garage

While the prospect of putting up lights can fill a person with anticipation and even creative discovery at finding new ways to make the house glow, taking them down and storing them is often just a chore. Still, it's a crucial one. Light sets have to come down; they aren't designed to face the weather all year. (Even if they could stay up all year, your neighbors would probably object.)

It's important to be careful in removing the lights. If you don't put them away properly, you'll start next year's decorating by facing a bunch of tangled wires and broken bulbs — which can seriously detract from your motivation.

First, take pictures of your lights. A visual record of where the lights went will help if you want to do a similar display (or avoid making the same mistakes) next year.

Before you take anything down, unplug it. There's no point to spending all of December in perfect safety from electric shock only to get electrocuted when it's all done. That sort of thing gets you laughed out of heaven.

Get a bunch of plastic bags. Label each bag with the name of each component and its location: "Icicle lights for front left rain gutter," "Clips for front left rain gutter," "Extension cord for front left rain gutter, "Extension cord for front yard tree," "Mini-lights for front yard tree branches," "Rope lights for front yard tree trunk," and so on.

As you take the components down, inspect them for the same problems that you sought out when you put them up. If you find burned-out bulbs, replace them. If you find cracked components, frayed wires, or other problems, throw the set away. Then buy a replacement set. You shouldn't have too much trouble getting one, since stores sell light sets at a discount in the after-Christmas season. If you can't find a replacement at the moment and have to wait for next year when holiday lights reappear in stores, jot down a note about the set — kind of lights, number of lights, and so on — and put the note in the bag that you've labeled for it. Next year, when you dig out your equipment to put up the lights, you'll have a note in the bag reminding you of what to buy.

But back to the components that you're not replacing, the ones that you're keeping for next year. There are lots of products that will help you store lights without tangling them into knots. You can wind strands of lights onto handheld reels about a foot long. For extra-long strands, Christmas lighting companies and hardware stores sell giant spools, like the ones for garden hoses.

But a cheaper tool is the humble paper-towel tube. Wrap a strand of lights around the tube, tuck the strands' ends into the tube's hollow interior, and tape the lights and tube together. For strands that run too long for a single tube, a long pole or broomstick will do.

After you wind the strands, label them in the same way that you labeled the bags. Put each component in the appropriate bag, and seal the bag to keep moisture and other elements out. Similarly label and bag every extension cord and all other accessories that had been connected to the strand. When you unpack them to set up next year's display, the labels will tell you which cords go with which strands.

Now, you're ready to put everything away. Put the bags full of lights and accessories in large plastic tubs with lids. If possible, have a separate tub for each group of lights and accessories — one tub for the lights that go on the roof, another tub for tree lights, another for walkway lights, and so on. Label each tub.

Put the tubs in a cool, dry place. And voila, you're ready for next year. Now, get some rest!

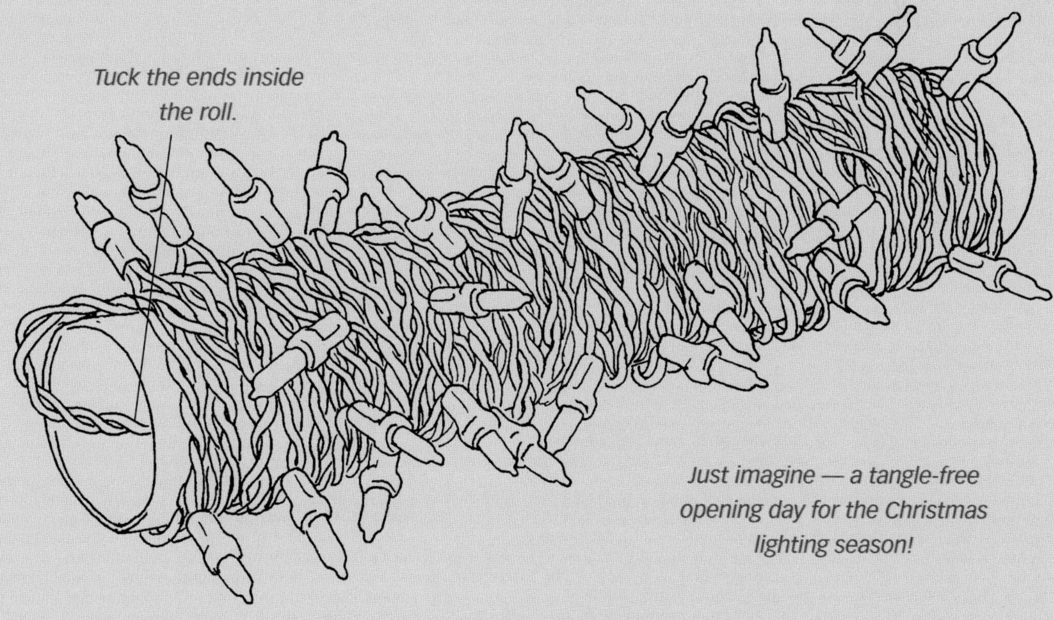

Just imagine — a tangle-free opening day for the Christmas lighting season!

Avoiding Disaster

Generally speaking, holiday lighting is a pretty safe activity. But when a few strands of lights strung up in the front hedges evolve to gargantuan displays of floodlight intensity, with wiring run amuck and not a spot of yard left to step in, a few safety precautions are, if slightly dull, still important to keep in mind.

- If you can't be home, don't turn on the display. Leaving a display unattended is an invitation to fire.
- Never touch a lit display. Whenever you need to work on your lights — to replace a burned-out bulb, check an extension cord for fraying, rearrange a light strand — turn them off and unplug them first.
- Unplug the entire strand before you replace any of its bulbs, unless you want a strong shock and Bride of Frankenstein hair. If it's unplugged, a strand can't send shocks through you.
- Replace burned-out bulbs as soon as possible. A dead bulb in a strand interferes with the proper flow of electricity. It's important to replace the bulb rather than just remove it; an empty socket is an invitation to children's fingers.
- Never force a three-pronged plug into a two-hole outlet.
- Use one long extension cord rather than several small ones. Keep cords away from metal, moisture, and hot places such as heaters, fireplaces, and furnaces.
- Keep cords and wiring out of the paths of home residents and visitors.
- Don't run extension cords from inside your house to an outdoor display. You risk damaging the cord (by people stepping on it or windows closing on it). Running cords in flammable indoor places, such as behind curtains or near wrapping paper, is just as dangerous. Instead, have an electrician install outlets outdoors.
- Keep pets and children from touching the lights. That chore may not be easy if you have lights draped over fences or running along walkways, but it's important. If you can't be sure that you can make kids and animals avoid the places where you put the lights, then don't put lights on those places.
- Don't let bulbs touch anything that turns to flame quickly and easily, like dry leaves or thin branches. This instruction may make tree lighting tricky, but it will prevent fires. If possible, turn any bulbs on branches upside down so that they point away from the branches and toward the ground. This arrangement will keep the bulbs' burning filaments from heating the branches and prevent moisture from settling in the bulbs' sockets.
- If you're decorating your front yard with lit-up Christmas trees, apply the same rules that you'd apply to indoor trees. Don't put electric lights on metal trees. Keep the bulbs from drying out the trees (and turning them into a fire hazard) by setting them in water, but don't let anything electrical get near the water. Anchor the trees (and anything else that you place on your property and light up) so that no sprinting kid or gusting storm can accidentally knock them down.

- As much as possible, keep your display away from moisture. Don't put lights near puddles or other sources of water. Place your outlets, plugs, cords, and other equipment in sheltered areas that stay dry during storms. Whatever you install, and wherever you put it, secure it tightly and keep it dry.

- If rain is coming, turn off and unplug the display. Keep the rain off of it by covering it — or as much of it as possible — with a tarp, plastic sheeting, or something else that's waterproof. Secure this shielding tightly so that it protects the display against wind; nobody wants to see a high gale wrench light strands off of eaves and gables or send the strands swinging wildly with every gust of wind. If you've attached lights to free-standing items like Santas or reindeer, take the items inside. You could cause unfortunate injuries (and maybe a crisis of faith) if a storm blows your plastic Nativity scene through your neighbor's front window.

If all of this seems daunting, remember that paying attention to it now will give you a more carefree experience when the lights are ablaze. So warily watch for dangers, carefully secure displays in only the safest places, and thoroughly double-check everything . . . but have fun!

THE NUTCRACKER
Ontario

Where to Go & What to Get

The true holiday lights enthusiast always wants more: more bulbs, more amps, more animation, and more information. If you hunger to suck up facts about holiday lights, hunt down places to shop, travel to extravagant lights displays, or otherwise satisfy your lust for everything you can get from winter incandescence, then keep reading. Like the holiday season itself, a paradise of merchandise retailers, travel destinations, and smart advice is waiting for you.

Metropolitan Tours

Truly magnificent lights displays can be found countrywide. However, many metropolitan areas are fortunate to host a grouping of such sites, which may all be visited in the course of one grand evening of lights touring. For more information about each of the lights displays listed here, turn to the following pages.

SAN DIEGO, CALIFORNIA

Coronado: Hotel Del Coronado

Del Mar: Del Mar Fairgrounds

San Diego: San Diego Bay Parade of Lights

SAN FERNANDO VALLEY, CALIFORNIA

Burbank: North Florence Street

Granada Hills: Ludlow Street

Reseda: Bertrand Avenue

SILICON VALLEY, CALIFORNIA

Fremont: Cripps Place neighborhood

Monte Sereno: Danielle Place

Palo Alto: Laguna Avenue

Sunnyvale: Lakewood Village neighborhood

PORTLAND, OREGON

Portland: Oregon Zoo, The Grotto, Columbia and Willamette Rivers Christmas Ship Parade

SEATTLE, WASHINGTON

Bellevue: Bellevue Botanical Gardens

Brier: Southwest 228th Place

Federal Way: Southwest 332nd Street

Seattle: Ballard neighborhood, Ravenna neighborhood

Tacoma: Port Defiance Zoo

PHOENIX, ARIZONA

Glendale: Downtown Glendale's Glendale Glitters

Phoenix: Desert Botanical Garden, Phoenix Zoo

Tempe: Mill Avenue's Fantasy of Lights

DENVER, COLORADO

Denver: Denver Botanic Gardens, Denver City and County Building, Denver Zoo, South Zenobia Street, Xcel Energy Parade of Lights

DALLAS–FORT WORTH, TEXAS

Arlington: Interlochen neighborhood

Dallas: Highland Park neighborhood

Fort Worth: Downtown Forth Worth Verizon Wireless Parade of Lights

AUSTIN, TEXAS

Austin: West 37th Street neighborhood, Zilker Park neighborhood

Johnson City: Blanco County Courthouse

Marble Falls: Lakeside Park

MINNEAPOLIS–SAINT PAUL, MINNESOTA

Inver Grove Heights: Dawn Avenue

Minneapolis: Downtown Holidazzle

St. Paul: Kellogg Park

West St. Paul: Hall Avenue

CHICAGO, ILLINOIS

Chicago: Magnificent Mile

Geneva: Cheever Avenue

Roselle: May Street

ST. LOUIS, MISSOURI

Ballwin: Woodland Crossing neighborhood

Belleville, Illinois: National Shrine of Our Lady of the Snows

Eureka: Jellystone Park

St. Louis: Tilles County Park

CINCINNATI, OHIO

Cincinnati: Cincinnati Zoo, Sharon Woods Park, North College Hill neighborhood

ATLANTA, GEORGIA

Atlanta: Buckhead neighborhood, Centennial Olympic Park, Stone Mountain Park

Lake Lanier Islands: Magical Nights of Lights

Marietta: Life University

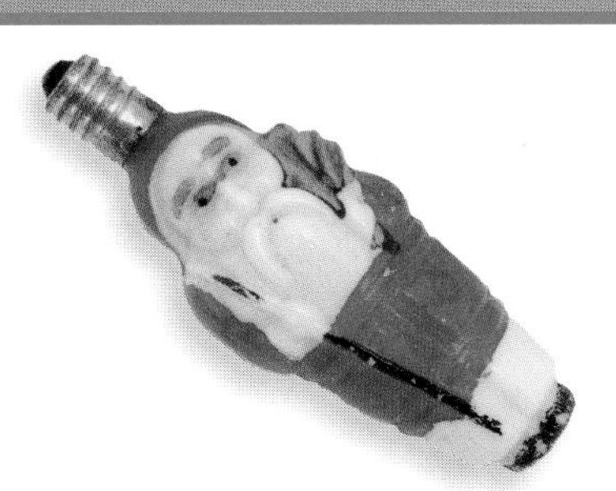

ORLANDO, FLORIDA

Orlando: Brandon Circle,Walt Disney World, Winter Haven, Cypress Gardens

MIAMI, FLORIDA

Fort Lauderdale: Intercoastal Waterway

Pinecrest: Southwest 119th Street

Sunrise: Northwest 132nd Avenue

WASHINGTON, D.C.

Centreville, Virginia: Bull Run Regional Park

Columbia, Maryland: Symphony Woods

Gaithersburg, Maryland: Seneca Creek State Park

Kensington, Maryland: Washington Temple of the Church of Jesus Christ of Latter-Day Saints

Manassas, Virginia: Lee Manor Drive

Upper Marlboro, Maryland: Watkins Regional Park

Wheaton, Maryland: Brookside Gardens

NEW YORK, NEW YORK

Manhattan: Central Park, Empire State Building, Macy's Department Store, Radio City, Rockefeller Center, Tavern on the Green Restaurant

BOSTON, MASSACHUSETTS

Boston: Quincy Market

Braintree: Eileen Drive neighborhood

Saugus: Lynn Fells Parkway neighborhood

Tewksbury: Carolina Road

Trips to the Light Fantastic

Traveler beware: Things change. Places that have a great display one year may have absolutely nothing the next. Some places start lighting up on Thanksgiving; others wait until it's nearly Christmas Eve. Some end on Christmas; others continue well into the new year. Before you travel, call ahead or check the appropriate website, if you can. If no such resources are available, take your chances, and good luck!

ALABAMA

Huntsville
Huntsville-Madison County Botanical Gardens
4747 Bob Wallace Avenue
256-830-4447
www.hsvbg.org
Galaxy of Light; 300 lighted exhibits.

ALASKA

Anchorage
West Anchorage neighborhood
91st Avenue near West Dimond Blvd.
Neighbors in this area try to outdo each other with big displays.

ARIZONA

Flagstaff
Little America Hotel
2515 East Butler Avenue
928-779-7900
More than a million lights.

Glendale
Downtown Glendale
Glendale Glitters festival; more than a million lights over 12 blocks.

Mesa
Arizona Temple of the Church of Jesus Christ of Latter-Day Saints
525 East Main Street
www.christmasfestival.org
Temple Garden Christmas Lights Festival; 50 life-size illuminated figures and 600,000 lights.

Phoenix
Desert Botanical Garden
1201 North Galvin Parkway
480-941-1225
www.dbg.org
Las Noches de Las Luminarias, with more than 7,000 luminarias.

Phoenix Zoo
455 North Galvin Parkway
602-273-1341
www.phoenixzoo.org
Zoolights, featuring more than two million lights.

Sedona
Tlaquepaque Arts & Crafts Village
State Highway 179, south of U.S. 89
928-282-4838
www.tlaq.com
Festival of Lights, a night lit by thousands of luminarias.

Tempe
Mill Avenue at Rio Salado Parkway
480-967-4877
www.millavenue.org (the local merchants association)
Fantasy of Lights: luminarias, parades, and other items.

ARKANSAS

Eureka Springs
Downtown Eureka Springs
Winter Lights, an event that lights up all of downtown.

Little Rock
State Capitol building
Woodlane and Capitol Avenue
A well-lit edifice that is part of the state-sponsored Trail of Lights, which leads visitors from one glowing municipal building to another.

CALIFORNIA

Burbank
North Florence Street
500 block
www.dicknorton.com/xmas/xmashome.html
www.wintersnowland.com
Here lie the homes of friends and rivals in excess Dick Norton and Keith LaPrath. The websites above offer photos of their displays.

Coronado
Hotel Del Coronado
1500 Orange Avenue
619-435-6611
www.xmasdel.com
About 50,000 lights lining this hotel.

Costa Mesa
Trinity Broadcasting Network
3150 Bear Street
714-708-5405
So many glowing lights that they sparked public protests.

Del Mar
Del Mar Fairgrounds
2260 Jimmy Durante Boulevard
www.sdfair.com
Del Mar Holiday of Lights, the West Coast's largest drive-through holiday light show.

Fremont
Cripps Place neighborhood
Near Nicolet Avenue
A neighborhood that collects donations for the Leukemia Society.

Granada Hills
Ludlow Street
17500 block
A house in this neighborhood sports more than 100,000 lights.

Huntington Beach
Huntington Harbor
714-969-3492 (the Visitors Bureau)
Huntington Harbor Cruise of Lights, one of California's largest boat parades.

Los Angeles
Griffith Park
Los Feliz neighborhood
213-485-5501 or 323-913-4688
www.dwplightfestival.com
Holiday Light Festival, a mile-long route with displays of holiday themes and Los Angeles landmarks.

Monte Sereno
Danielle Place
15000 block
Aliens, spaceships, and 100,000 lights can be found in this neighborhood.

Newport Beach
Newport Harbor
949-729-4400 (the Chamber of Commerce)
www.christmasboatparade.com
Christmas Boat Parade, with more than 150 lighted boats.

Oakland
Picardy Drive neighborhood
A 60-year-old neighborhood tradition; lights strung from home to home.

Palo Alto
Laguna Avenue
3600 block
Visitors will find at least one house in this neighborhood with more than 10,000 lights, plus reindeer on the roof.

Reseda
Bertrand Avenue
6400 block
Unusual decorations abound here, including Santa's Living Room and Santa riding a cow.

Riverside
Mission Inn
3649 Mission Inn Avenue
909-784-0300
www.missioninn.com
Two million lights on more than 200 figures.

San Diego
San Diego Bay
www.sdparadeoflights.org
Bay Parade of Lights, with sailboats, yachts, and everything in between.

Sunnyvale
Lakewood Village neighborhood
This neighborhood runs a contest for best display.

Union City
Clover Street
34700 block
The Teixeira and Peetz families: friendly competitors who try to outlight one another.

COLORADO
Denver
Denver Botanic Gardens
1005 York Street
720-865-3500
www.botanicgardens.org
Blossoms of Light, with more than 20 acres of illuminated ponds, pathways, and flower displays.

Denver City and County Building
1437 Bannock Street
Riotous yet dignified and awe-inspiring shafts of red and green.

Denver Zoo
City Park, East 23rd Avenue near Colorado Boulevard
303-376-4800
www.denverzoo.org
Wildlights, a two-mile route featuring animated images of animals.

South Zenobia Street
One of Colorado's most impressive residential displays can be found here, just north of West Alameda Avenue.

Xcel Energy Parade of Lights
Downtown Denver
303-478-7878
www.denverparadeoflights.com
More than a million lights on some of the country's fanciest floats.

CONNECTICUT
Hartford
Goodwin Park
Maple Avenue between Jordan Lane and Brown Street
860-343-1565
www.holidaylightfantasia.com
Holiday Light Fantasia, a two-mile drive through animated displays including angels, kings riding camels, and the Statue of Liberty.

DELAWARE
New Castle
Red Lion Road
1000 block
Featuring the famous Faucher home, with more than 600,000 lights.

FLORIDA
Citrus Park
Rawls Road
5100 block
A musical Christmas home, with a singing snowman, a dancing Santa, and lights synchronized to music.

Coconut Creek
Tradewinds Park
3600 West Sample Road
954-968-3880
Holiday Fantasy of Lights, with more than a million lights on 65 displays.

Fort Lauderdale
Intercoastal Waterway
954-767-0686
www.winterfestparade.com
Winterfest Boat Parade, with 100 boats traveling over a 10-mile course.

Juno Beach
Ridge Road
1700 block
A well-lit grouping of houses.

Orlando
Brandon Circle
10000 block
Neighbors here compete for the wildest display.

Walt Disney World
Disney-MGM Studios
407-824-2222
www.disneyworld.com
Osborne Family Spectacle of Lights.

Pinecrest
Southwest 119th Street
6800 block
www.clotxmas.com
The Clot Family Christmas: 650,000 lights, plus animated figures.

St. Augustine
Downtown St. Augustine
904-829-1711 (the Visitors Bureau)
www.nightsoflights.com
Nights of Lights, with more than a million lights throughout the city.

Sunrise
Northwest 132nd Avenue
1000 block
A pair of homes lit up inside and out with displays.

Winter Haven
Cypress Gardens
2641 South Lake Summit Drive
800-282-2123
Garden of Lights Holiday Festival, with more than five million lights over Christmas and Alpine scenes.

GEORGIA
Atlanta
Buckhead neighborhood
4200 block of Powers Ferry Road NW
Over a million lights on a home here.

Centennial Olympic Park
285 International Boulevard
www.centennialpark.com
404-222-7275
Holidays in Lights, with more than 80,000 lights in displays including giant rainbows, penguins in an igloo, and elves tossing packages.

Stone Mountain Park
Exit 8 off of Interstate 78
770-498-5702
www.stonemountainpark.com
A Southern Christmas, with 200 lights displays.

Lake Lanier Islands
Across the islands
800-840-5253
www.lakelanierislands.com
Magical Nights of Lights; more than 6.5 miles of animated displays.

Marietta
Life University
1269 Barclay Circle
Lights of Life, with two million lights on displays that include 60-foot Santa, reindeer crawling over a building, and a reindeer flight school.

Pine Mountain
Callaway Gardens
U.S. Highway 27
800-225-5292
www.callawaygardens.com
Fantasy in Lights, a five-mile drive through scenes such as March of the Toy Soldiers, Swan Lake, and Twelve Days of Christmas.

HAWAII
Honolulu
Honolulu Hale (City Hall)
530 South King Street
Mele Kalikamaka, with Santa giving a "hang loose" sign.

ILLINOIS

Alton

Rock Spring Park
College Avenue at Rock Spring Drive
618-466-8858
Celebration of Christmas, with more than 150 displays.

Belleville

National Shrine of Our Lady of the Snows
442 South De Mazenod Drive
618-397-6700
Way of Lights Christmas Display; a million lights over a 1.5-mile route.

Chicago

Magnificent Mile
Michigan Avenue, from Oak Street to Wacker Drive
www.themagnificentmile.com
Magnificent Mile Lights Festival; more than a million lights on display, plus an annual parade.

Galena

All over town
815-777-9050 (the Chamber of Commerce)
www.galena.org
Night of the Luminaria, with more than 5,000 lights in bags.

Geneva

Cheever Avenue
800 block
www.twasthenightbefore.com
The Parcell home features lights synchronized to music, plus dozens of character figures.

Roselle

May Street
Also known as Candy Cane Lane; it's so bright that it reportedly has caught the attention of flight crews out of O'Hare Airport.

IOWA

Keokuk

Rand Park
Orleans Avenue at North 14th Street
319-524-5433
www.cityofchristmas.org
City of Christmas, with more than 250,000 lights and 100 displays.

KANSAS

Great Bend

Various places all over town
877-427-9299 (the Visitors Bureau)
www.greatbend.com
Trail of Lights, with a lit-up zoo, park, and Christmas Fantasy Village.

KENTUCKY

Lexington

Kentucky Horse Park
4089 Iron Works Parkway
859-233-4303 or 800-678-8813
www.kyhorsepark.com
Southern Lights, featuring stars, horses, rainbows, and other displays.

LOUISIANA

Alexandria

Argonne Boulevard
5200 block
www.MagicChristmas.org
The Monkhouse home offers lit-up toys, trees, and a train.

Natchitoches

Cane River Lake
800-259-1714
www.christmasfestival.com
Festival of Lights, a 300,000-bulb event that draws more than 100,000 visitors a year.

New Orleans

City Park
Wisner Boulevard at City Park Ave.
504-483-9415
www.neworleanscitypark.com
Celebration in the Oaks, which attracts more than 30,000 cars and 100,000 pedestrians; includes fairy-tale homes in its Storyland section.

Fairmont Hotel
123 Baronne Street
504-529-7111
Lobby with a canopy of 70,000 lights.

MARYLAND

Annapolis

Annapolis Harbor and Spa Creek
www.eastportyc.org
Eastport Yacht Club Lights Parade, featuring dozens of boats.

Sandy Point State Park
1100 East College Parkway
410-974-2149
Lights on the Bay, with 60 displays along a 2.5-mile drive.

Columbia

Symphony Woods
10475 Little Patuxent Parkway
410-740-7666
Symphony of Lights, with more than 70 light sculptures.

Flintstone

Rocky Gap State Park
12500 Pleasant Valley Road
301-777-2139
www.MtReflections.com
Mountain Reflections, featuring dozens of large illuminated displays.

Gaithersburg

Seneca Creek State Park
11950 Clopper Road
301-924-2127
Winter Lights Festival, with more than 200 illuminated displays.

Kensington

Washington Temple of the Church of Jesus Christ of Latter-Day Saints
9900 Stoneybrook Drive
Festival of Lights, with more than 300,000 lights.

Ocean City

Northside Park
125th Street in the Bayside area
410-289-2800 (Ocean City Public Relations department)
www.ococean.com
Winterfest of Lights, with more than 800,000 lights, a drive-through nautically themed show, and hundreds of displays.

Sharpsburg

Antietam National Battlefield
Route 65 between Routes 34 and 68
301-432-5124
Antietam Illumination, with 23,000 luminarias to commemorate the soldiers who fell at Antietam's Civil War battleground.

Upper Marlboro

Watkins Regional Park
301 Watkins Park Drive
301-218-6700
Festival of Lights, with more than 400,000 lights covering an entire train station, a gigantic tree, and other items.

Wheaton

Brookside Gardens
1800 Glenallen Avenue
301-962-1453
Garden of Lights, with botanical displays and fantasy figures.

MASSACHUSETTS

Attleboro

La Salette Shrine
947 Park Street
508-222-5410
Christmas Festival of Lights, with more than 200,000 lights.

Boston
Quincy Market
1 Faneuil Hall Marketplace
617-338-2323
www.faneuilhallmarketplace.com
A large, colonial-style building lined in white lights.

Braintree
Eileen Drive neighborhood
A group effort where all the decorations coordinate to dazzling effect.

Holliston
Fatima Shrine
101 Summer Street
508-429-2144
A walk-through filled with lit-up symbols of Catholicism.

Saugus
Lynn Fells Parkway neighborhood
An elaborately lit group of houses.

Springfield
Forest Park
Sumner Avenue off of Route 83
413-787-6440
www.brightnights.org
Bright Nights, with more than 300,000 lights on display in Seuss Land, Noah's Ark, North Pole Village, a Hanukkah menorah, and a tribute to Kwanzaa.

Tewksbury
Carolina Road
200 block
A home here has 100,000 lights on display, including a rooftop train, animated deer, and a helicopter in a tree.

MICHIGAN

Battle Creek
Downtown, riverfront, and the zoo
800-397-2240 (the Visitors Bureau)
www.battlecreekmich.com
International Festival of Lights, featuring more than a million lights and symbols of the world's religions.

Frankenmuth
Bronner's Christmas Wonderland
25 Christmas Lane
800-255-9327
www.bronners.com
Featuring Christmas Lane, a half-mile-long drive-through lights display, as well as the Silent Night Memorial Chapel, a replica of the original chapel in Oberndorf, Austria.

MINNESOTA

Inver Grove Heights
Dawn Avenue
7800 block
A home with 100,000 lights, a Santa House, and Santa driving a '57 Chevy.

Minneapolis
Downtown; Nicollet Mall
612-376-7669
www.holidazzle.com
Holidazzle Parade, a march of lighted trains, toys, and people.

St. Paul
Kellogg Park
Kellogg Boulevard West at Cedar St.
The world's largest Salvation Army kettle, with more than 20,000 lights.

West St. Paul
Hall Avenue
1000 block
Santa and the missus can be found here in a dancing light show.

MISSOURI

Ballwin
Woodlyn Crossing neighborhood
www.faszl.com
Faszl's Digital Christmas, a showplace of animated lights.

Branson
Branson Lakes area
800-214-3661 (the Visitors Bureau)
www.ozarkmountainchristmas.com
Branson Area Festival of Lights, running 15 miles and including five million bulbs, in displays ranging from Santa riding a dinosaur to a partridge in a pear tree and a spouting whale.

Silver Dollar City
399 Indian Point Road
800-475-9370
www.silverdollarcity.com
Old Time Christmas, an event that lights up this amusement park.

Eureka
Jellystone Park
Fox Creek Road near Allenton Road
636-938-5925
www.eurekajellystone.com/santa
Santa's Magical Kingdom, featuring more than two million lights on displays including Candy Cane Factory and Santa's Acrobatic Elves.

Kansas City
Country Club Plaza
Broadway between 47th Street and Ward Parkway
816-753-0100 or 816-221-5242
www.countryclubplaza.com
More than 200,000 bulbs light the edges and rooftops of the Country Club Plaza shopping district.

Kansas City Zoo
6800 Zoo Drive
816-513-5700
www.kansascityzoo.org
WildLights, with dozens of light sculptures and hundreds of thousands of bulbs.

St. Louis
Tilles County Park
Litzsinger Road at McKnight Road
314-615-4386
Winter Wonderland, with more than a million lights.

NEBRASKA

Omaha
Gene Leahy Mall
Farnam Street, between 10th and 14th Streets
www.holidaylightsfestival.org
Holiday Lights Festival, with about a million lights on display.

NEW HAMPSHIRE

Bedford
Plummer Hill Road
Near Highway 114
A home that looks like a lit-up gingerbread house.

Plaistow
Elm Street
Near Main Street
The Reed home, thoroughly covered in lights.

NEW JERSEY

Old Bridge
Gaub Road
Near Matawan Old Bridge Road
Giant toy soldiers, Hanukkah décor, airplanes, a train, and more.

NEW MEXICO

Albuquerque

Rio Grande Botanic Gardens
2601 Central Avenue Northwest
505-764-6200
www.cabq.gov/biopark/garden
River of Lights, with more than a million bulbs.

San Felipe de Neri Parish
2005 North Plaza
505-243-4628
Dozens of luminarias along the church's walkways and rooftops.

Santa Fe

Inn of Loretto
211 Old Santa Fe Trail
505-988-5531
www.hotelloretto.com
Luminarias line the rooftops of a hotel that looks like an ancient Indian cliff dwelling.

NEW YORK

Albany

Washington Park
Madison Avenue at New Scotland Avenue
Capital Holiday Lights, a drive-through that benefits the Albany Police Athletic League.

The Bronx

Bronx Zoo
Fordham Road at the Bronx River Parkway
718-367-1010
Holiday Lights Festival; 150 animated animal sculptures and 500,000 bulbs.

Brooklyn

Dyker Heights neighborhood
1000 and 1100 blocks of 84th Street
Homes decorated in shamelessly high style.

Manhattan

Central Park
Midtown between 59th and 110th Streets
212-310-6600
www.centralparknyc.org
Holiday Lighting, a grand event with the Charles A. Dana Discovery Center turned into an electric gingerbread house.

Empire State Building
Fifth Avenue at 34th Street
Changes color with the seasons.

Macy's Department Store
Herald Square, 151 West 34th Street
Elaborate window displays.

Radio City
1260 6th Avenue, between 50th Street and 51st Street
www.radiocity.com
Gigantic illuminated trees, toy soldiers, and wrapped gifts.

Rockefeller Center
5th Avenue and 47th Street to 7th Avenue and 51st Street
www.rockefellercenter.com
A huge tree and angel sculptures.

Tavern on the Green Restaurant
Central Park at West 67th Street
www.tavernonthegreen.com
Trees and bushes covered in lights.

Wantagh

Jones Beach State Park
Off of Wantagh Parkway South
516-785-1600
www.tommyhilfigerjonesbeach.com/hl
Holiday Light Spectacular, a 2-mile stretch of a million lights on more than 120 displays, including dancing fish in Santa hats.

NORTH CAROLINA

Carolina and Kure Beaches

Various sites on Pleasure Island
800-222-4757 (the Visitors Bureau)
www.islandoflights.com
A holiday parade, lit-up holiday flotilla, and tour of local homes.

Holly Springs

Windward Pointe neighborhood
A group of householders who compete fiercely to create their displays.

McAdenville

Throughout the town
704-824-3190 (the town clerk)
www.mcadenville-christmastown.com
Virtually the entire town lights up.

New Bern

Highway 117
Between New Bern and Vanceboro
The Wetherington abode, home of Christmasaurus Rex.

OHIO

Cincinnati

Cincinnati Zoo
3400 Vine Street
513-281-4700
www.cincyzoo.org
Festival of Lights, with more than two million lights over the zoo's 72 acres.

Sharon Woods Park
Route 42 south of Interstate 275
513-769-0393
www.holidayinlights.com
A drive-through display with more than 250,000 lights.

North College Hill neighborhood
2000 block of West Galbraith Road
A home here displays more than 500 illuminated figures and dozens of decorated trees.

Cleveland

Nela Park
1975 Noble Road
General Electric's holiday lights show, with hundreds of thousands of bulbs.

Public Square
Downtown Cleveland
More than a million lights on famous Cleveland landmarks.

OREGON

Coos Bay

Shore Acres State Park
13030 Cape Arago Highway
541-888-3732 or 800-824-8486
www.coosbay.org
Shore Acres Christmas Lights; more than 200,000 lights strung over trees, bushes, and buildings.

Portland

Columbia and Willamette Rivers
www.christmasships.org
Christmas Ship Parade, a tradition going back nearly 50 years.

The Grotto
Sandy Boulevard and Northeast 85th Avenue
503-261-2400
www.thegrotto.org
The Grotto Festival of Lights, with about 500,000 lights decorating this Catholic sanctuary.

Oregon Zoo
4001 Southwest Canyon Road
503-226-1561
www.zooregon.org
Zoolights, featuring about half a million lights on a variety of displays.

PENNSYLVANIA

Indiana Township

Hartwood Acres
Saxonburg Boulevard north of Harts Run Road; just a short distance from Pittsburgh
877-548-3874
Eckerd Celebration of Lights; more than 3miles of displays using more than 2 million lights.

Kennett Square
Longwood Gardens
Route 1 south of Exit 52
610-388-1000
www.longwoodgardens.org
A Longwood Gardens Christmas, with more than 300,000 lights on dozens of illuminated trees and bushes.

SOUTH CAROLINA
Charleston
James Island County Park
871 Riverland Drive
843-795-7275
www.holidayfestivaloflights.com
Holiday Festival of Lights, featuring more than a million lights.

TENNESSEE
Chattanooga
Rock City Gardens
1400 Patten Road
706-820-2531
www.seerockcity.com
Enchanted Garden of Lights, featuring more than half a million lights in 25 holiday scenes.

Gatlinburg, Pigeon Forge, and Sevierville
Throughout all three towns
800-267-7088 or 800-343-1475
www.smokymountainwinterfest.com
Smoky Mountain Winterfest, a set of lighting events that take over all three towns plus the neighboring Dollywood theme park.

Memphis
Graceland
3765 Elvis Presley Boulevard
800-238-2000
www.elvis.com
Two million lights on Elvis's home, courtesy of Jennings Osborne.

Nashville
Opryland Hotel
2800 Opryland Drive
615-889-1000
www.oprylandhotelnashville.com
A Country Christmas, with millions of lights on trees and shrubbery.

TEXAS
Arlington
Interlochen neighborhood
About 200 homes, all lit up.

Austin
West 37th Street neighborhood
One of the best-lit neighborhoods in the United States.

Zilker Park neighborhood
The Trail of Lights, a well-organized collection of lit-up homes and gigantic displays.

Dallas
Highland Park neighborhood
Especially Beverly Drive and the streets nearby
An upscale area that decorates with taste but no restraint.

Fort Worth
Downtown Fort Worth
817-336-2787
www.fortworthparadeoflights.org
Verizon Wireless Parade of Lights, with more than 100 entries.

Johnson City
Blanco County Courthouse
101 East Pecan Street
A building with more filigree than a wedding cake.

Marble Falls
Lakeside Park
307 Buena Vista
830-693-4449 (the Chamber of Commerce)
Christmas Walkway of Lights, featuring a tunnel of lights plus Santas twirling a lariat, running a steamship, and water skiing.

Marshall
Harrison County Courthouse
200 West Houston Street
A building famous for the white lights that line its roof, windows, and trees.

San Antonio
River Walk
210-227-4262
www.thesanantonioriverwalk.com
Texas's famous shopping and strolling area, with more than 100,000 lights; the annual Holiday River Parade & Lighting Ceremony kicks off the season.

VIRGINIA
Centreville
Bull Run Regional Park
7700 Bull Run Drive
703-709-5437
www.miracleoflights.com
Miracle of Lights, featuring 2 miles of lights with more than 200 displays arranged by themes including "Planet Holiday," where aliens celebrate Christmas.

Manassas
Lee Manor Drive
Off of Shannon Lane
www.christmaswonderland.org
The Jezioro Christmas Wonderland, with about 40,000 lights.

Virginia Beach
Virginia Beach Boardwalk
800-822-3224
Chick-Fil-A Holiday Lights at the Beach, featuring 400,000 lights in more than 250 nautical and holiday displays.

WASHINGTON
Bellevue
Bellevue Botanical Gardens
12001 Main Street
425-452-2750
www.bellevuebotanical.org
Garden d'Lights, with bulbs dripping off of trees, bushes, arches, and trellises, plus a class in light design.

Brier
Southwest 228th Place
3700 and 3800 blocks
This neighborhood of about a dozen homes is one of the brightest places in the region.

Federal Way
Southwest 332nd Street
2200 block
A home here features more than 100 figures (including an 8-foot snowman), plus a bubble machine.

Leavenworth
Downtown Leavenworth
509-548-5807
www.leavenworth.org
A Bavarian village with lights on every rim and edge.

Seattle
Ballard neighborhood
7000 block of 32nd Avenue NW
Visitors will find a North Pole village with nearly 20,000 lights.

Ravenna neighborhood
Park Road
www.candycanelane.org
Candy Cane Lane, a decades-old tradition of finely crafted home displays.

Tacoma
Port Defiance Zoo
5400 North Pearl Street
253-591-5337
www.pdza.org
Zoolights, with light sculptures of exotic animals and holiday scenes.

WEST VIRGINIA
Wheeling
Ogelbay resort
Route 88 North, four miles off of Interstate 70 at exit 2A
304-243-4000 or 800-624-6988
www.oglebay-resort.com
Winter Festival of Lights, a 6-mile drive through illuminated displays.

WISCONSIN
Milwaukee
Downtown Milwaukee
414-220-4700
www.milwaukeedowntown.com
Milwaukee Holiday Lights Festival, decorating the entire downtown.

Canada

ALBERTA

Edmonton

Hawrelak Park
9930 Groat Road
Billed as the largest drive-through Christmas lights theme park event in Canada, with over 375 displays.

Sylvan Lake

49th Street
Between 45th and 47th Avenues
www.sylvanlights.com
The Lawrence North Pole display, with elaborate lighting effects.

BRITISH COLUMBIA

Vancouver

Carol Ships Parade of Lights
Coal Harbour waterfront
www.carolships.org
A 40-year-old tradition including more than 80 boats and 150,000 lights.

MANITOBA

Winnipeg

Power Smart Festival of Lights Parade
Downtown Winnipeg
Sponsored by Manitoba Hydro; floats, lights, and fireworks.

ONTARIO

Niagara Falls

Downtown and elsewhere
905-356-6061 or 800-563-2557
Winter Festival of Lights, with lighted parades and other holiday attractions.

Rockwood

Rockwood Farmers' Santa Claus Parade of Lights
www.blahs.on.ca
Holiday parade mounted on tractors and other farm vehicles.

QUEBEC

Montreal

Santa Claus Parade
Saint Catherine Street
www.christmasinmontreal.com
A classic parade that winds its way down the main drag of Montreal, kicking off the holiday season.

SASKATCHEWAN

Saskatoon

The Enchanted Forest
Saskatoon Forestry Farm Park; 1903 Forest Drive (off Attridge Drive)
306-975-3382
Also billed as the largest drive-through Christmas lights theme park event in Canada. A 2.2-kilometer drive, with over one million lights and 1,000 images.

Lighting Resources

Lights Suppliers

You can never have too much information about holiday lights — or enough lights, for that matter. These prominent companies sell lights and lights-related items: bulbs, controllers, light displays, installation supplies, and so on. Some carry all of these items, while others carry a more narrow selection, but they all have a variety of goodies. Some of them even offer full-service design, installation, and dismantling of holiday lights displays.

All American Christmas Company
P.O. Box 208
384 Broyles Street
Sparta, TN 38583
Phone: 931-836-1212
Fax: 931-836-2002
Web: www.AllAmericanChristmas.com

Alsto's
P.O. Box 1267
Galesburg, IL 61402
Phone: 800-621-8258 or 309-343-6181
Fax: 800-522-5786
Web: www.alsto.com

Bethlehem Christmas Lights
2291 East Route IL18
Streator, IL 61364
Phone: 217-351-8861
Web: www.bethlehem-lights.com

Betty's Christmas House
212 West Main Street
Streator, IL 61364
Phone: 815-673-5824
Fax: 815-672-4495
Web: www.bettyschristmashouse.com

Brite Star
2900 South 20th Street
Philadelphia, PA 19145
Phone: 215-271-7600
Fax: 215-467-9222
Web: www.britestar.com

Bronner's Christmas Wonderland
25 Christmas Lane
Frankenmuth, MI 48734
Phone: 989-652-9931
Web: www.bronners.com

Cheesy Lights
339 West Antietam Street
Hagerstown, MD 21740
Phone: 800-248-0645 or 301-766-0166
Fax: 301-766-0215
Web: www.cheesylights.com

Christmas Depot
750 Broadway
Bayonne, NJ 07002
Phone: 877-353-5263
Fax: 201-437-3218
Web: www.christmasdepot.com

Christmas Done Bright
1805 Winfield Dunn Parkway
Sevierville, TN 37876
Phone: 888-453-0599
Web: www.christmasfactory.com

Christmas Lights, Etc.
7455 Northampton Court
Cumming, GA 30040
Phone: 678-455-5445
Fax: 866-790-0253
Web: www.christmaslightsetc.com

Christmas Moon
P.O. Box 433
East Brookfield, MA 01515
Phone: 508-981-7808
Web: www.christmasmoon.com

Christmas Trim Discount
Web: www.christmastrimdiscount.com

Crystal Valley International
3124 Northwest 16th Terrace
Pompano Beach, FL 33064
Phone: 305-947-8700
Web: www.crystalvalleyintl.com

Davmark, Inc.
P.O. Box 3227
Spring, TX 77383
Phone: 877-478-7085 ext. 4500
Fax: 281-528-6020
Web: www.davmark.com

December Lights
P.O. Box 1628
Dawsonville, GA 30534
Phone: 706-579-1665
Fax: 706-265-2198
Web: www.decemberlights.com

Holiday Lights & Magic
820 Chandler Grove
Hermitage, TN 37076
Phone: 800-954-5511
Web: www.holidaylightsandmagic.com

Holiday Litesource
808 8th Street
Lubbock, TX 79401
Phone: 800-762-2855
or 806-744-7744
Fax: 806-744-4871
Website: www.litesource.com

Holiday Marketplace
254 J.P. Taylor Road
Henderson, NC 27537
Phone: 800-548-0626 or
252-438-6111
Fax: 252-438-4815
Web: www.holidaymarketplace.com

Holiday Presence
848 North 1430 West
Orem, UT 84057
Phone: 800-640-9627
Fax: 801-222-9362
Web: www.holidaypresence.com

Illumibrite
4423 Beach Drive East
Port Orchard, WA 98366
Phone: 360-769-2215
Web: www.illumibrite.com

Improvements Catalog
5876 Mayfield Road
Mayfield Heights, OH 44124
Phone: 800-542-4467 or
440-442-7074
Web: www.improvementscatalog.com

Lori's Lighted D'Lites
17803 Northeast Highway 301
Waldo, FL 32694
Phone: 877-647-4906 or
352-468-2904
Web: www.lorislighteddlites.com

Marshall Moody Display
2910 North Stemmons Freeway
Dallas, TX 75247
Phone: 800-627-0123 or
214-631-5444
Fax: 214-631-4609
Web: www.marshallmoody.com

Nida Lighting
3919 Parkway Lane, Suite 6
Hilliard, OH 43026
Phone: 800-761-6432 or
614-529-9902
Fax: 614-529-9903
Web: www.nidagroup.com

Novelty Lights
1630 West Evans Avenue, Suite K
Englewood, CO 80110
Phone: 800-209-6122 or
303-671-0533
Fax: 303-671-5700
Web: www.noveltylights.com

PartyLights
4317 Montrose Boulevard
Houston, TX 77006
Phone: 713-529-9540
Fax: 713-529-0224
Web: www.partylights.com

Sexy Bloomers
P.O. Box 252
Palmyra, NY 14522
Phone: 315-597-5330
Fax: 315-597-6892
Web: www.sexybloomers.com

Simply Lighting
P.O. Box 870
Sicklerville, NJ 08081
Phone: 888-876-9892 or
856-262-2632
Fax: 856-262-1630
Web: www.simplylighting.com

Sival, Inc.
3350 Scott Boulevard, #2001
Santa Clara, CA 95054
Phone: 800-777-8667 or
408-492-1391
Fax: 408-492-1393
Web: www.sivalinc.com

Smarthome, Inc.
16542 Millikan Avenue
Irvine, CA 92606
Phone: 800-762-7846 or
949-221-9200
Fax: 949-221-9240
Web: www.smarthome.com

Specialty Suppliers

Some companies offer only a few items for lights enthusiasts. They're not the only groups that sell the items listed below — some of the "general store" organizations listed above may carry them as well — but they may offer expertise that a generalist wouldn't have.

Animated Lights and Controllers

Animated Lighting
7304 West 130th Street, Suite 100
Overland Park, KS 66213
Phone: 913-402-0700
Fax: 913-402-0722
Web: www.animatedlighting.com

Light Bug
2800 South 24th Street West
Muskogee, OK 74401
Phone: 918-683-3469
Fax: 918-686-8289
Web: www.lightbug.com

Figures and Light Sculptures

Blowmold Central
26 F Congress Street, #143
Saratoga Springs, NY 12866
Web: www.blowmoldcentral.com

Brite Ideas Decorating
3852 Farnam Street
Omaha, NE 68131
Phone: 888-200-5131 or
402-553-1178
Fax: 402-553-7402
Web: www.briteidea.com

A Christmas Light Company
1949 Red Cedar Street
Toms River, NJ 08753
Phone: 732-929-1300
Fax: 732-929-2322
Web: www.christmas-lites.com

Grand Venture
250 West Wylie Avenue
Washington, PA 15301
Phone: 888-746-5350 or
724-222-9601
Fax: 724-222-9622
Web: www.grandventure.com

Holiday Lighting Specialists
100 West Holiday Lane
Tonkawa, OK 74653
Phone: 800-627-4146 or
580-628-4146
Fax: 580-628-4833
Web: www.holidaylights.com

Key Access/Affluent Living Catalog
1139 South Placentia Avenue
Fullerton, CA 92831
Phone: 888-612-7400 ext. 337
Web: www.keyaccess.com

Paul's Outdoor Decorations
634 York Road, PMB 135
Warminster, PA 18974
Fax: 215-343-0815
Web: www.paulsoutdoordecor.com

Union Products
511 Lancaster Street
Leominster, MA 01453
Phone: 978-537-1631
Fax: 978-537-0050
Web: www.unionproducts.com

LED Lights

Backwoods Solar Electric System
1395 Rolling Thunder Ridge
Sandpoint, ID 83864
Phone: 208-263-4290
Web: www.backwoodssolar.com

Holiday Creations
5161 East Arapahoe Rd., #330
Littleton, CO 80122
Phone: 303-694-1121
Fax: 303-721-9878
Web: www.foreverbright.com

Music and Broadcasting

Broadcast Warehouse Ltd
P.O. Box 32901
Wimbledon SW19 8FZ
England
Phone: 011 44 0-208 540-9992
Fax: 011-44 0-208 540-9994
Web: www.broadcastwarehouse.com

Panaxis Productions
P.O. Box 130
Paradise, CA 95967
Phone: 530-873-9100
Fax: 530-873-9200
Web: www.panaxis.com

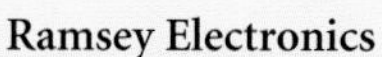

Ramsey Electronics
793 Canning Parkway
Victor, NY 14564
Phone: 800-446-2295
Fax: 585-924-4886
Web: www.ramseyelectronics.com

Rope Lights

Food Service Direct
905 G Street
Hampton, VA 23661
Phone: 757-245-7675
Web: www.foodservicedirect.com

The Holiday Lights Community

Even when thousands of miles separate them, holiday light enthusiasts aren't lonely, or at least don't have to be. Thanks to the Internet and other resources, a lighter can see what his colleagues several time zones away are doing. Below are some of the best means to that end.

Christmas Lighting and Displays Webring
Web: v.webring.com
Just search for the webring by name.

Christmas Lights Chatroom
Web: www.planetchristmas.com
PlanetChristmas sponsors a very good chat room for lighters. Look for the link on the PlanetChristmas home page.

The Christmas Lights Page
Web: lights.fcpages.com
The website will take you into the Christmas Lights Net Ring.

PLUS: PlanetChristmas Lights Up Symposium
Web: www.planetchristmas.com
The website offers information on PLUS, a conference of sorts for holiday lighters. Just look for the PLUS link.

Index

Page numbers in *italics* indicate a photograph or illustration.

Interior Photography Credits

© K. Yamashita/Pan Stock/Panoramic Images 2–3; © Steve Dunwell/Image Bank/Getty 6–7; Ed Judice 7; © K. Yamashita/Pan Stock/ Panoramic Images 8–9; © Andy Caulfield/ Image Bank/Getty 10; © Royalty-free/CORBIS 10–11; © Eric Schmidt/Masterfile 12–13; © Richard Cummins 14; Charlie Newham/ Alamy 14–15; © Randy Faris/CORBIS 16; © Danny Lehman/CORBIS 16–17; © W.J. Scott/Robertstock.com 18; © Philip Harvey/CORBIS 19; © Chuck Savage/CORBIS 20–21; © Michael St. Maur Sheil/CORBIS 22t; James Oakley Photography, courtesy of The Highlander Newspaper 22b; © Justin Morrison 23tl; © Richard Cummins 23r; © Richard Hamilton Smith/CORBIS 23bl; Ed Judice 23m (ornament); © W.J. Scott/Robertstock.com 24l; © Macduff Everton/CORBIS 24r, 24i, and 25l; © Lynn Seldon 25m; © Justin Morrison 25r; The Advertising Archive Ltd./The Picture Desk 26l; © 1999–2003 William G. Nelson/www.oldchristmaslights.com 26r; © Hulton-Deutsch Collection/CORBIS 27; © Carl D. Walsh/Aurora and Quanta 28l; Ed Judice 28r; © James Baron/The Image Finders 29; Ed Judice 30; © Henley/CORBIS 30–31; © Kevin Fleming/CORBIS 32–33; The Clot Family 35l (large photo and insets); Ed Judice 35r (light bulbs); Ron Lister/ www.Christmas-Wonders.homestead.com 36; Andy and Barb's Christmas Wonderland/Photography by Reflective Images 37; ©Steve Dunwell/Image Bank/Getty 38–39; © K. Yamashita/Pan Stock/Panoramic Images 40–41; Keith A. LaPrath 40i; Dick and Pam Norton and Family/www.nortonswinterwonderland.com 41ti; The Washburne Family 41b; Image State/Alamy 42; Magic Christmas, Alexandria, LA 44; Toni Willis 45; © Nick Gunderson/ CORBIS 46; Earl Hargrove 47tl, 47tr, and 47br; Ed Judice 47bl; © W.J. Scott/Robertstock.com 48–49; Ron Lister/www.ChristmasWonders.-homestead.com 49li; © Corinne Dune 49mi; Jim Langone/Spirit of Springfield 49ri; © J. Irwin/Robertstock.com 50; Barefoot John 51b; Ed Judice 51t (ornament); The Faszl Family/www.faszl.com 52tl, 52tr, and 52m; © Mark Segal/Panoramic Images 52b; The Faszl Family/www.faszl.com 53t; Ed Judice 53b; The Faucher Family 54–55; Ed Judice 56; © Jim Gipe 57; © Carrington Weems 58–59; The Boston Globe/Joanne Rathe 60 and 61; © Shirlee Simon-Glaze 62; © Jacob Dobkin 63; Ed Judice 64t; © NY-CJPG.com 64b, 64–65, and 66; © Carrington Weems 68–69; © Corinne Dune 70l and 70r; Giles Prett 70t (skeleton light); © Carrington Weems 71; © Kevin Fleming/CORBIS 72l; Ed Judice 72r; © 2002 Southern Living, Inc. 74; © Wernher Krutein/Photovault 75; The Boston Globe/Joanne Rathe 76–77; © Sandy Felsenthal/CORBIS 78tl; Ed Judice 78tr; © Carrington Weems 78b, 79, and 80; © 1999–2003 William G. Nelson/www.old-christmaslights.com 81; Courtesy of the Gatlinburg Department of Tourism 82i; © Gary W. Carter/CORBIS 82b; © Greg Pease/Stone/Getty 83; Ed Judice 85t; Dieter Melhorn/Alamy 85b, 86t, and 86i; Don Adams/courtesy of Leavenworth Chamber of Commerce 88–89 and 89b; © Owaki-Kulla/CORBIS 90–91; © Elvis Presley Enterprises 92 and 93t; © 1999–2003 William G. Nelson/www.oldchristmas-lights.com 93b; John Kuntz/© 2002 The Plain Dealer 94l; Ed Judice 94r; Jim Langone/Spirit of Springfield 95; Courtesy of the Albuquerque Biological Park 96l; © Charles Crust 96–97; © Richard Cummins 97; © Reuters NewMedia Inc./CORBIS 98; © The Purcell Team/CORBIS 99; © Big Bamboo Stock Photography 100; © Kaz Chiba/Getty 101t; © Nicole DuPlaix/National Geographic/Getty 101b; © Sandra Baker/Image Bank/Getty 102–103; © Royalty-free/CORBIS 103m; Image100/Alamy 103i; © Shaun Egan/ Stone/Getty 104; Courtesy of Milwaukee Convention and Visitor's Bureau 105i; Silver Dollar City 105tr; © James Randklev/Taxi/ Getty 105b; Pawel Libera/Alamy 106; © Wilfried Krecichwost/Image Bank/Getty 107t; Ed Judice 107b; Courtesy of the Denver Zoo 108t, 108b, and 109tl; Courtesy of the Phoenix Zoo 109tr; © John McAnulty/CORBIS 109b; © Bachmann/Image Finders 110b; NOTMC/David Richomond 110i; NOTMC/ Paul Combel 111; © Nevada Wier/CORBIS 112; © Gene Peach/Stone/Getty 113l; © Philip Harvey/CORBIS 113tr; © Bob Krist/CORBIS 113br; Courtesy of Mesa Convention and Visitor's Bureau 114; Jim Langone/Spirit of Springfield 115l and 115r; © Mark Segal/ Panoramic Images 116; © Greg Ryan and Sally Beyer 117; Courtesy of Bronner's Christmas Wonderland 118l; © Frank S. Balthis 118r; © Kevin Fleming/CORBIS 119tl; Ed Judice 119tr; © D. Logan/Robertstock.com 119b; © Ron Sanford/CORBIS 120–121; © Michael DeYoung/CORBIS 122b; © Rick Sauders/ Index Stock 122ti; © Jeri Gleiter/ Taxi/Getty 122ri © Henryk T. Kaiser/Trans-parencies 123; © Buddy Mays/CORBIS 124–125; © Bettmann/CORBIS 125r; © Carrington Weems 126i; © Justin Morrison 126–127; © Rick Sauders/Index Stock 128tl; © Andre Jenny/Focus Group/PictureQuest 128tr; © Richard Cummins 128bl; © Justin Morrison 128br; © Garry Gay/Image Bank/Getty 129tr; © Carrington Weems 129br; © Chip Simons/Taxi/Getty 130; © Nick Vedros & Assoc./Stone/Getty 131; © John Henley/CORBIS 132–133; Ed Judice 134t and 134b; C. Squared Studios/Photo-disc/Getty 136; Ed Judice 138 (large bulb); Giles Prett 138–139 (small bulbs); © Royalty-free/CORBIS 139tr; © Jim Gipe 139br; © Adam Jones 141; © Gary Rhijnsburger/ Masterfile 142; Ed Judice 143, 144, and 146t; Barefoot John 146b; © Jim Craigmyle/ CORBIS 147t; © Randy Faris/CORBIS 147b; © J. Irwin/Robertstock.com 148; Andy and Barb's Christmas Wonderland/Photography by Reflective Images 149; © Carrington Weems 150; © Carl Stimac/Image Finders 152; Giles Prett 153; © Mike Mullen 154; Andy and Barb's Christmas Wonderland/ Photography by Reflective Images 156; Ed Judice 158; © Victor Englebert 160–161; Ed Judice 161 (ornament); Courtesy of Bronner's Christmas Wonderland 162; Ed Judice 164–165 (ornaments); © Richard Hutchings/CORBIS 165r; © Mark Segal/ Panoramic Images 166–167; Ed Judice 169, 170, and 171; © 1999–2003 William G. Nelson/www.oldchristmaslights.com 172; Courtesy of Bronner's Christmas Wonderland 173; Ed Judice 174; © 1999–2003 William G. Nelson/www.oldchristmaslights.com 176; Ed Judice 177t; Courtesy of Bronner's Christmas Wonderland 177b; © 1999–2003 William G. Nelson /www.oldchristmaslights.com 178; Ed Judice 180.

Key: t = top, b = bottom, l = left, r = right, m = middle, i = inset